Make Meetings Work

I would like to dedicate this book to all my friends, colleagues and teams over the years.

I would also like to thank Liz Pilcher for all her help and support in writing this book.

....

Credits

Front cover: © terex – Fotolia

Back cover: © Jakub Semeniuk/iStockphoto.com, © Royalty-Free/Corbis, © agencyby/iStockphoto.com, © Andy Cook/iStockphoto.com, © Christopher Ewing/iStockphoto.com, © zebicho – Fotolia.com, © Geoffrey Holman/iStockphoto.com, © Photodisc/Getty Images, © James C. Pruitt/iStockphoto.com, © Mohamed Saber – Fotolia.com

Make Meetings Work

Karen Mannering

Hodder Education
338 Euston Road, London NW1 3BH

Hodder Education is an Hachette UK company

First published in UK 2011 by Hodder Education

This edition published 2011

www.hoddereducation.co.uk

Typeset by Ce tree Publisher Services

Printed in Gre

Contents

Meet the author

Welcome to *Make Meetings Work*!

Meetings are inevitable. They figure heavily in all walks of life and create a forum for providing information, holding discussions and making decisions. Whether you hold meetings in your office or attend international summits, the meeting is a place where a certain etiquette is essential.

As someone who has both worked in different areas of business and trained staff in meeting skills and minute taking, I understand that information about these skills is not always available in a format that is easily accessible and helpful, and this is my reason for writing this book.

During my career I have seen it all – meetings where no one actually turns up to others where the room is so full that participants have to perch on the table or even stand throughout. I have also witnessed poor etiquette where people are sending text messages under the table, and others openly eating their packed lunch during the discussion.

Not everyone enjoys attending meetings but they remain the fastest and most efficient way of both communicating a uniform message to lots of people and gaining people's views, and for this reason they are here to stay. Whether you take part in the meetings of your local parish council or an informal support group, how to run a meeting, behave in a meeting, construct minutes, and chair meetings are all essential skills for anyone wishing to move projects forward or forge a career in business.

There are numerous simple tips and tricks that can save you time and energy, and ensure your meeting runs with polished precision – and it is these I want to share with you. After all, meetings should be productive time-savers, not boring time-wasters, and any time invested in them should reap dividends.

Whatever kind of meeting you are involved in, you will gain more from the experience by having a greater knowledge of how meetings are run effectively and where you can create impact.

In one minute

If you have only one minute, think about the meetings in your life and try to gain a broad overview. How successful are the meetings you are currently attending?

Grab a piece of paper now and write down a list of all the meetings you attend. Now give them a mark out of ten for importance and then another mark out of ten for effectiveness. For example:

Meeting	Importance	Effectiveness
Team meeting	8	4
Project progress meeting	8	8
Social club meeting...	4	7

and so forth.

Now look at the meetings that are the most important and ask yourself:

- ▶ Are they also the most effective?
- ▶ What could I learn from this?
- ▶ If they are not effective, whose fault is this?
- ▶ Is there anything I personally could do to help?

It may be that some of our most important meetings are not run effectively, and it is these that we should concentrate on first. This book will help you to do just that.

Introduction

Meetings can take up a huge amount of our time but have we ever really considered whether we make the most of their potential? Many people see them as a necessary evil rather than considering the positive properties they bring. Perhaps that is because we are not using them in the right way and therefore not benefitting from them as we should.

This book aims to take you on a journey through every aspect of meetings. It is presented in four parts:

▶ **Part one** gives you the complete background to meetings – what they are, the different types of meetings (and when to use which type) and finally how you organize and administer a meeting.
▶ **Part two** assumes that you are now a participant attending a meeting. It details how you should prepare for the meeting, the behaviour and planning that is expected of you, how to present material or be a speaker in a meeting, and then what to do when the meeting is over.
▶ **Part three** is centred on minute taking and covers appropriate formats, the role of the minute taker, how to structure and produce the minutes and, finally, their distribution.
▶ **Part four** is aimed at those who chair meetings and takes you from deciding that you need a meeting through to the follow-up. There is also a useful section on troubleshooting with answers to many often-raised questions.

Throughout the entire book you will find:

▶ **insight boxes** – these provide you with an additional insight into a subject
▶ **tips** – these are additional tips that can either provide short cuts or really make a difference
▶ **'try this' boxes** – these will be points where you will be given the opportunity to reflect on the material or undertake an action
▶ **case studies** – this will be an example situation.

Here's to a future where meetings become a valuable and welcome part of your business or life!

Part one

Part one

The meeting

1

What are meetings for?

In this chapter you will:
- *consider the purpose of meetings*
- *appreciate the need for different meetings to match different needs*
- *understand why and how some meetings fail to deliver.*

What is the function of a meeting?

You may view meetings as a delight, a place where decisions are made, or try to avoid them like the plague because they take up too much of your time. Whatever your view, meetings are here to stay, as they perform a valuable role as a forum for discussing useful information and making informed decisions.

Meetings are the mainstay of business and can take the form of:

▶ **an information point** – where many people can hear the same information in the same way and everyone feels included (e.g. a team meeting)

▶ **a discussion group** – where information may be discussed or aired, and many people can contribute to the input (e.g. a group coming together to discuss a childcare plan)

▶ **a problem-solving session** – where many people gather to solve key business problems (e.g. a meeting to discuss the best way to generate additional income from current sales)

▶ **a decision-making forum** – where decisions of any scale are formally taken (e.g. a meeting with contractors to agree the terms of a new contract)

Therefore a meeting does more than get people together; it can be the launch pad for new ideas (the idea of the Post-it note was generated during a meeting), a short cut to gaining clarification over issues, and a way of agreeing decisions. In essence, it should save time because, if everyone is present, the information/discussion only has to happen once. Speed is also generated by the Chair of the meeting, keeping it on track and ensuring that the agenda is followed. (Of course not all meetings keep to time or structure, but we will discuss this later.)

Within public sector organizations there are three other reasons for meetings:

1 **Democracy** – decisions should not be made unless there are representatives from all parties present, and only after all information, views and feelings are heard. Unfortunately, this can result in the long-winded and multiple meetings that local government is renowned for; nonetheless it is necessary to capture all viewpoints.

2 **Transparency** – major decisions and the acceptance of new policies need to be delivered in the public arena to ensure transparency and reduce mistrust. This means that some of the main council meetings will be open to the public and there is public access to all of the minutes from local government meetings. If the public are to retain their trust in public sector officers and officials, local government has to allow many of its more crucial meetings to take place in an open forum where officers can be heard and challenged.

3 **Historical documentation** – all meetings (and of course their accompanying minutes) tell a story of a decision or action, but in local government terms these become historical data. For example, if a historian wanted to research why Brunel was not allowed to build a bridge in one particular place, all they have to do is search the relevant council's archives for the minutes of that planning meeting. Similarly, if someone was adopted as a child, they may wish to find out what policies were in place in the council at that time, and the meetings that were held that led to adoption by a particular family taking place. Many councils and public bodies are being challenged as to the decisions they have made both in the present day and in the past. It is the minutes from meetings that provide some of the data and detail that will be used in the research.

Meetings can be regular or a one-off situation. They may be light-hearted in their tone – as in a meeting to arrange a social calendar – or they could be serious – such as a meeting to discuss an office move. They may involve everyone you know, as in a team meeting, or you may be faced with complete strangers. They can be short, and they can be long. Whatever form and tone the meeting takes, it is important that it presents itself in the right way and that all these aspects are considered.

In business, meetings are for moving the company forward, a process or framework on which the business relies to enable future growth. Meetings can be described as being forward thinking in that, while they may discuss the background or history to an event, the reason for this is to influence the future and aid in developing a solution. Business needs meetings, whether large board meetings or informal one-to-ones.

Insight

Think for a minute – what type of meetings does your organization or business run? What purposes do they have? How much are you contributing towards making each meeting a success (even when it is not your meeting)?

What happens at meetings?

Meetings are not just static events or time-wasters; they are a useful conduit towards action. People come together to consider and debate issues that should resolve in some outcome or action. Therefore those attending the meeting should be the right people to ensure that this actually happens.

Meetings are usually structured into **items** (see more under 'A typical meeting cycle' below), and each item can be one of the following:

▶ **Information** – this is information given to the group to provide knowledge. It may or may not lead on to a decision being made or a problem being solved. An example of information being given in a stand-alone format is when someone provides everyone with an overview of a new piece of legislation that is being introduced. When you know information is being given, you need to pay attention but recognize that your input is not required (except for clarifying points).

▶ **Request for a decision** – this is when a decision has to be made. There could be some information given. In the example given above, someone presented a new piece of legislation. However, the person may now need to push for a decision from the attendees as to the exact date they will implement the legislation.

▶ **Problem solve** – problem solve topics may take a little longer. They are used when the speaker wants to stimulate as many ideas from the meeting as possible. Meetings are a great place to bring people together who have a common purpose to look at ways of solving problems. Quite simply, with so many more brains around the table there is a higher likelihood of a solution being found.

Items can be taken in any order – not all meetings stick to the order of the agenda. This can be because of people's time issues (for example, if someone needs to leave early and there is a particular item they wish to hear), or perhaps someone has decided that, since the agenda was drawn up, the pre-information from another item is needed before the current one can be dealt with. There may also be some new items that were not on the agenda that need to be covered urgently, and so may need to be squeezed in. Similarly, some other items may be dropped, perhaps because the presenter cannot attend for some reason, because the project was not finished in time, or simply because there is not enough time. Items like these can be rolled forwards into future meetings.

Different roles in meetings

A meeting can range from a couple of people to a roomful. If you are having a very small, informal meeting, it is likely that there will not be different roles, but any meeting over four people needs managing through the use of differently attributed roles.

Typically, meetings will have the following:

THE CHAIR (OR CHAIRPERSON)

Their job is to keep the meeting on track. They may be a part of the meeting or they may be completely separate. The role of the Chair is set out in greater detail in Part four, but essentially it is to ensure that the meeting sticks to the agenda, moves swiftly, and that everyone has an opportunity to speak. The Chair will interject to move topics on or ask people to stop and clarify certain points. The person undertaking this role needs to be able to scan the room for body language and notice where and when people want to speak. The Chair also has to be quite firm in identifying actions to be highlighted at the end of each agenda topic and make sure decisions are recorded. Following on from the meeting, the Chair also has a crucial part in ensuring the minutes are correct and distributed.

THE MINUTE TAKER

Although not all meetings have a separate minute taker, all but the most informal meeting will need minutes taken. The minute taker is there to provide a written representation of the meeting that can be distributed later. When a meeting is over, the minutes are the only record of what was discussed and the outcome, and therefore it is important to ensure they contain sufficient detail for anyone not able to attend to be able to follow them and see the implications for their part of the business. If the meeting is a large negotiation, each party may have their own minute taker so that the final minutes can be compared for any errors in interpretation. Minute taking is covered in detail in Part three of this book.

THE TIMEKEEPER

Not every meeting has a separate timekeeper and this role may be doubled up with another role. Essentially the job of the timekeeper is to ensure that the meeting runs to time and covers all the topics. This can be crucial: if there are six items to cover in the meeting and each one overruns by just ten minutes, this will add another hour to the meeting. The timekeeper will have the full permission of everyone present to interject if the topics are not being covered fast enough or to interrupt if the agenda looks like it may not be covered in time.

GUEST PRESENTERS

The meeting may need guest presenters. They are people who will not be present for the entire meeting but will come into the room at certain points and present their information or topic. It may be that they present formally (a media presentation, for example), or they may just join the table and talk through the information they have to share.

DEVIL'S ADVOCATE

At some meetings there may be someone acting as 'devil's advocate'. This means that they will look at the situation from the other perspective. This is to ensure that everyone is aware of the negatives as well as the positives. For example, if someone was describing the benefits of a new scheme, the devil's advocate might point out that the meeting should also identify the disadvantages of introducing the scheme.

ATTENDEES

All meetings need contributors who will attend and actively take part in the meeting discussions. Usually attendees fall into two categories: regular attendees and invited attendees. Regular attendees make up the meeting at every session, while invited attendees attend only when specifically invited. This may be because some of the agenda items cross over into their subject areas or perhaps because they are influential and have a view or opinion to contribute that would affect any decision.

Set up to fail?

When you reflected on the meetings you have attended, which I suggested in 'In one minute' at the beginning of this book, you may have thought: 'Well, not all meetings I attend seem to go so smoothly and productively.' It is true that not all do, and there could be many reasons for this, so let's look at some of them:

► **No decision can be made** – this is usually an outcome of a meeting where the wrong people are present or where there is a lack of information. For decisions to be made there needs to be attendees with the right level of authority to take decisions or allocate funds to certain projects. Without this, meetings will go around in circles and end with everyone having to return to their manager to sanction any action. They also need access to all the information required. If someone has to go back to their team to discuss the issue or for more information, the decision will have to be delayed.

► **Meetings that overrun** – this can happen when meetings have been poorly managed either by the person who has tried to push too much onto the agenda, or by the Chair/timekeeper who is allowing each item or speaker to overrun. If each item overruns for just a few minutes, the cumulative effect is either a very late meeting or one where attendees start drifting off to other appointments.

- ▶ **Meetings that are rushed** – these have also been poorly managed. However, the problem here is that the full consequences of each item cannot be explored within the time allotted, and therefore decisions are rushed or no clear decisions are made.
- ▶ **Meeting is dominated by one person** – this can happen when the Chair is weak. It is desirable that, after a meeting, everyone should feel that they were involved and have contributed to the meeting – allowing one person to dominate the proceedings will thus have a severe effect on everyone else. The other attendees may feel that there is no point in joining the discussion as only one person's opinion seems to count. The Chair has to ensure that everyone is heard and that there is the opportunity for all to contribute.
- ▶ **Confused and rambling** – this can be the outcome when the meeting has no structure or purpose. Perhaps there was no agenda or focus for the meeting. Believe it or not, the reason for some meetings is that people think that they *should* hold a meeting – never mind whether it is relevant to the situation or even necessary!

Size matters

As mentioned earlier, meetings can be any size from two people upwards. However, size does matter. If you are seated around a conference table, then you are looking at a maximum size of around 20 people. When numbers grow larger than this they become difficult to control by the Chair as well as to minute. Large groups of people tend to split easily into subgroups and the Chair might find that there are several meetings going on within one meeting! This is compounded by the fact that human nature dictates that we tend to sit next to either our friends or the person we came in with. This behaviour makes us feel very comfortable – so comfortable in fact that we find we can chat away easily to the person we know and ignore the meeting altogether. Meetings involving large groups of people need certain considerations if such situations are to be avoided.

Where the meeting is a public one (perhaps to discuss the planning application for a new supermarket in the area) and you anticipate large numbers, chairs are often laid out in rows so that everyone faces forward and the Chair can run the meeting like a conductor instructs an orchestra. Minute takers can also have problems with large groups as they find it difficult to know the names of everyone and record who said what. The Chair needs to be very aware of this and work with the minute taker accordingly.

So is the 'Holy Grail' small-sized meetings? Not necessarily. The right-sized meeting is one where the correct people are present, however many that may be. Small meetings can be easier to minute but in smaller meetings people tend to talk more quickly and there is less debate. They use verbal abbreviations a lot more and therefore a knowledge of the background to any discussion becomes more necessary. The point here is that you need to take size into consideration when you are planning your meeting so that you can organize it accordingly for optimum results.

A typical meeting cycle

Meetings can take any form but a typical format is as follows:

1 **Welcome by the Chair** – the Chair usually welcomes everyone, particularly any guests who may be present. At this point they may also deal with any 'housekeeping' points such as where the toilets are or whether there will be a break for refreshments and so on. The Chair may also confirm everyone's availability to check who can stay for the full meeting.

2 **Previous minutes** – minutes from the previous meeting should have been circulated in advance and therefore everyone should have a copy either in paper form or on their laptop / electronic pad. It is usual to rush through these in the assumption that everyone should have read them thoroughly before the meeting. Everyone is expected to say if there are any aspects that have not been correctly recorded.

3 **Review of the agenda** – the agenda is reviewed by the Chair to…
   ▶ clarify that everyone who needs to be present, is there
   ▶ check that there are no late entries
   ▶ confirm the time that any visiting speakers or presenters should arrive
   ▶ calculate the time for each agenda item (so that the entire length of the meeting can be calculated).
If there are too many items on the agenda or it looks like the meeting is going to overrun, the Chair may make a decision to cut the meeting into two or to carry some agenda items over.

4 **Items or topics** – at this point the meeting actually starts and the items are taken in the order agreed earlier. It is good practice to allocate a time for each speaker by each agenda item as this gives them a 'slot' of time to allocate to their subject – but not all meetings do this.

5 **Any other business (AOB)** – AOB is traditionally a 'catch all' for small items that emerged after the agenda was distributed. However, overuse can lead to lazy planning and the meeting overrunning. If attendees think they can put anything in the AOB section, then they will not bother to come up with topics or items for the agenda – after all they can always add them in the meeting. This can become the start of sloppy planning.

6 **Round-up/conclusion/confirmation of key actions** – depending on how the meeting is run, before the meeting ends the Chair may wish to make a concluding statement and agree any outcomes or actions with the relevant parties, especially key ones that perhaps link to the outcome of a project.

7 **Date of next meeting** – unless the meeting is a regular one (e.g. every week or every second Tuesday in the month), the Chair will generally ask everyone to agree the date of the next meeting. It is usually done at the meeting itself because it is generally understood that attendees will have come prepared with their diary or electronic organizer so that they can schedule in any actions. The next date can be arranged via email after the meeting, but this can become confusing when only certain attendees can make some dates and not others.

8 **Thanks** – generally the meeting ends with the Chair thanking everyone for attending.

9 **Minutes** – these follow on after the meeting has finished. Ideally you should expect them within one week of the meeting but, because they rely on the Chair signing them off, this may take a little longer. Everyone should check the minutes for accuracy before noting any personal actions and filing them for the following meeting.

Not all meetings will include every one of these 'steps' but many meetings will follow a very similar format. Having a format to your meeting gives it structure and ensures all areas are covered. Whatever your format, it needs to be helpful rather than restrictive.

KEEP IN MIND...

1 Meetings are a hugely important way of making decisions.

2 If the meeting is not going well, it may be that the format does not match the purpose.

3 Meetings are about more than the information they contain. They are also a great opportunity for networking.

4 Consider the size of your meeting – too big and it might be unworkable.

5 Recognize that a meeting is a valuable management tool that costs money – use the time wisely!

6 Attend with an open mind and a resolution to contribute.

7 Be prepared to take on a challenging role in meetings. Many meetings benefit from having a 'devil's advocate' present.

8 If the meeting appears to be failing, look for clues in body language.

9 Make sure you express your views clearly and assertively so that you are heard.

10 Whatever your role, commit to making the meeting enjoyable and productive.

2

Different types of meetings

In this chapter you will:
- *discover several different types of meetings*
- *consider the impact different types of meetings have on the format*
- *learn how to decide on the best format for your meeting.*

Formal and informal meetings

There are many different types of meetings to suit all manner of different situations. Every organization will have its own character and you will need to work within what is appropriate for your business.

In Chapter 1 we looked at a number of different types of meeting and now we need to examine these more carefully since this has a bearing on a number of considerations such as:

▶ how the meeting is perceived
▶ who is invited
▶ the level of confidentiality
▶ whether you need to incorporate roles into the meeting.

Meetings can be either formal or informal, and this can be dictated by the subject or even the person (or company) holding the meeting. For example, a meeting to decide the right family to foster a child would be formal as there are legal implications – here the formality is determined by the subject. However, if you are calling a meeting to debate who should be the lead in a number of different projects, you may yourself decide the level of formality the meeting should have. Some managers might decide that it should be formal in case there are any future arguments over who was assigned which project, but some other managers might consider an informal meeting best as they like to maintain an informal atmosphere in their team.

Formal meetings are identified through:

- ▶ a dedicated minute taker being present
- ▶ a strong Chair
- ▶ a fixed agenda.

Informal meetings are identified through:

- ▶ an attendee taking the minutes
- ▶ more of a 'discussion'-type atmosphere
- ▶ a more flexible agenda.

Although you may not have any control over the status of your meeting, there are benefits for each style:

Benefits of a more formal meeting	Benefits of a more informal meeting
You are very focused on the outcome and therefore the meeting can move swiftly	You can flex and change the items being discussed, including the timescale of the meeting itself
Everything is recorded by a dedicated minute taker and so you are free to take part in the meeting without worrying about note taking	Everyone can relax and have a joke, and it can be a part of informal team building
There may be allotted times for contribution and so the agenda moves along at a pace	The agenda can switch and change to suit everyone's diary (and you may stay only for your item)

Business meetings

Meetings are often places where business takes place, whether that is discussing a contract, debating terms and conditions, or negotiating a deal. However, business meetings have other levels that need recognizing:

- ▶ It is at business meetings that you are seen 'performing'.
- ▶ It is in business meetings that you may find yourself in front of other influential staff who you might otherwise rarely meet.

Let's look at those two points in detail, starting with the first one. When we are at work we are judged not only on our outcomes – for example the success of the projects we manage – but also on how we operate. How well do you articulate? Are you good at explaining complex ideas and concepts? How are your manners with other people? How do you manage difficult behaviour and situations? A meeting gives you every opportunity to demonstrate these skills – skills that are highly prized by managers. We have all been in meetings where someone has lost their temper and shown themselves to be out of control – is this the sort of person you would like in your team? Meetings can certainly bring out all our character traits for all to see... and others to judge.

The second point builds on this. Depending on the type of business you work for, you may not have access to senior managers or even see them regularly. In large organizations their office may even be in another building, or on a separate floor, and if you wanted to impress them (let's say for a promotion) you probably have little access to them. However, senior members of staff often attend meetings, and this could be your place to shine. I have known several people gain a promotion from being observed during a meeting and then being 'earmarked' as demonstrating impressive skills.

Insight

Think about your own behaviour in meetings – could you be displaying an aggressive stance that you may find effective in obtaining your goals, but which others present find uncomfortable and which will do you no favours in the future?

Team meetings

What makes a team cohesive rather than a group of individuals all working together in one room? The answer is that they share common goals. They may all have different jobs and responsibilities but they are working towards a collective vision or idea and they share the same results. How is that idea or vision communicated and sustained? Through the team meeting of course!

Team meetings vary considerably in style but they tend to fall into our earlier categories of formal or informal. The style may also be dictated by other factors such as:

- **Where everyone is based** – if your team is on the road (as in the case of sales reps, for example) they may meet only periodically for team meetings, as opposed to those sitting opposite each other every day in the office. When people meet only periodically it is important that they feel part of the team, and the point of a regular team meeting is to address this. However, this might also cause additional problems as you may find they need time to chat and bond before the meeting – the type of chat people engage in when they see each other daily. If this is the situation, you may have to allow some time for this.

- **The number of people in the team** – as a rule of thumb, the more people present the more formal your team meeting will need to be. A strong Chair is needed to manage larger numbers to prevent fragmentation and subgroups forming. Smaller groups may need less management, but even with a group of four the Chair will need to make sure the team meeting remains in focus, as it can easily drift into a pseudo coffee morning.

- **What type of work is undertaken** – team meetings will be very different for a group of solicitors than for a manager in charge of shop staff, or a doctor on a ward. In some cases, the team meeting will be reflective ('Let's look at how many cases each of us tied up last month') and, in other situations, more immediate ('It will be busy tonight in Accident and Emergency and I want to talk about how we can work best as a team to deal with the expected volume').

- **How often they meet** – team meetings can range from daily meetings to quarterly meetings. How often you meet will also have an effect on the length of the meeting and the items on the agenda. If meetings are too regular, you may find that there is not enough to say, or risk repetition. Not often enough and you will have to plug the gap with other mechanisms for sharing information such as emails, notice boards, memos and intranet bulletin boards.

- **The culture of the team** – each team has a distinct culture, and that usually means 'the way we do things around here'. It might be that the way the team meeting is run, or how often it meets, has been dictated by a previous manager or even the team itself. Remember, if it is not fit for purpose, it is never too late to challenge outdated ideas and make changes.

Specialist meetings

Specialist meetings are meetings set up to achieve some particular goal – for example a meeting specifically set up to discuss your insurance payment, or to bring parties in a negotiation together. In other words, a one-off meeting that is not part of your usual stream of business meetings.

It is highly possible that in specialist meetings not all parties have met each other before. This might necessitate some introductions at the beginning, to inform everyone not only as to the names of those present but also the company they are representing and their reason for attending. This will enable everyone to know where each person is coming from (figuratively) and the stance they might take. It is highly likely that there will be a set agenda, as this kind of meeting will be focused on resolving issues and moving things forwards.

Although everyone should strive to be polite, as it is unlikely that you will all meet again (unlike in a team meeting or regular business meeting), there may be some lively behaviour that needs to be kept in check. For example, depending on the situation, these meetings may become heated or even fraught with emotion. Perhaps a lot is at stake for all parties, and for this reason it is very likely that a minute taker will be present to record the proceedings and the outcome.

Legal meetings

Legal meetings might include anything from meeting your solicitor to sign important documents for a house purchase, to receiving legal advice – or even discussing a course of action concerning a court case. Therefore the level of formality may be variable and so might the need for a witness. For domestic cases it would be unlikely for a minute taker to be present but, if the meeting were to decide on a large building project, it is likely that the other party would want to minute the proceedings and therefore may provide their own minute taker (who would, of course, copy everyone in).

A word of warning! Legal meetings by their nature are focused on detail and protocol, and will include a fair amount of legal jargon. Legal secretaries are trained to work with this jargon, but it might prove a challenge for a visiting note taker.

On some occasions it might be a case of my legal team meeting versus your legal team – in other words, legal representation on both sides. When this happens it is advisable to have a pre-meeting with your own legal team, but then allow your legal representative to state the case on your behalf. In this situation, they are best placed to argue your case, using the correct language, than you are.

Legal meetings tend to be more formal, but that is mainly because of the nature of the material – not necessarily because of the personalities in the room.

One-to-one meetings

On occasions you may need to have one-to-one meetings either with your own manager or with other people. In this situation the dynamic is very different. The mood may be jolly or reflective but there is no getting away from the intensity. In a one-to-one meeting there is literally nowhere to hide. You can't sit back and hope that someone else will contribute or skirt around questions; suddenly the spotlight is on you, whether it's to make a comment or to laugh at a joke.

One-to-one meetings can be formal or informal. You might be discussing your personal targets for the coming year in one meeting, and your preferences for the Christmas lunch in another. Although there may be an agenda, it is highly unlikely that there will be a minute taker, although someone might be present to take notes if the meeting concerns a disciplinary issue.

There are some benefits to one-to-one meetings over larger meetings. Let's look at the benefits of each:

Benefits of one-to-one meetings	Benefits of larger meetings
Fewer people should mean a faster conclusion	More brains around the table can mean more ideas
Confidential discussions can take place	Transparent practice – everyone can take part and hear what is being discussed
Builds a personal relationship between the two participants	You may be able to be more honest as you will not specifically set up a relationship with the Chair
Can be called quickly – literally whenever the participants are free to meet	Having a lead-in time allows for personal preparation

KEEP IN MIND...

1 The style of your meeting will depend on whether it is formal or informal.

2 Business meetings are a great way of working out the finer details and making agreements.

3 Never underestimate your own performance in business meetings – you are being watched, too!

4 Regular team meetings help teams to focus on how they can support the business in the best possible way.

5 Never be afraid of suggesting a rethink of your team meeting – just because something has always been done that way does not mean it has to continue.

6 If you are attending a legal meeting, make sure you have a grasp of any specialist language before you attend.

7 One-to-one meetings may still have an agenda.

8 Specialist meetings should not be 'business as usual'.

9 Always take your own notes in meetings. Do not rely 100 per cent on another person taking meaningful minutes.

10 If you need to take someone else to the meeting, inform the Chair (or person in charge) in advance.

3

Organizing a meeting

In this chapter you will:
- **find out how to set up a meeting**
- **consider the elements that contribute towards its success**
- **learn how to structure the agenda.**

Deciding the purpose and/or focus

So, you are about to call a meeting? Great, but what is it about? If your meeting does not have a purpose or focus, it will quickly become a talking shop – fine for a bit of gossip but not taken seriously. Neither will you be taken seriously as a manager/Chair or organizer – I'm sure you will agree that wouldn't be your intention.

Let's think about it another way. You want me to come to your meeting. I have a lot of urgent work right now and you say, 'I understand that you are busy but you must come – it's important.' Do you think I would bother to make time in my (choc-a-bloc) schedule for something that you have said is 'important' but where I have no notion of the subject? 'No,' I would most likely say. 'Tell me what it's about and I will judge whether I need to be there or not.' In other words, people like to know *why* they are being invited to meetings and *what* they are expected to contribute when they get there. Then *they* will decide whether the meeting is important. The higher up the organization the meeting is, the more this attitude becomes evident.

Busy managers are also more inclined to attend meetings if they know that:

▶ their contribution is valued
▶ their input will be noted

▶ a concrete decision will emerge from the meeting (in other words, that it is not just a discussion).

The 'nightmare' scenario is that no one (or any key deciders) turns up to the meeting, rendering it a waste of time. (And if they didn't accept your original invitation, they certainly won't turn up to a rerun!)

The **purpose** and the **focus** must therefore always be explicit. Let's define these two terms:

▶ The **purpose** is why you are having the meeting (for example – 'Meeting to discuss the new structure for the HR department, and to plan Phase One'). A purpose adds an air of urgency to an agenda since it implies action.
▶ The **focus** is what the meeting will concentrate on (for example – 'The focus for this meeting will be the IT requirements in HR for the next 12 months'). Stating a focus allows the people attending to think through the issues and come armed with questions and information – even if the meeting is only to discuss the issues and there is no concrete outcome.

You may decide to have both a purpose and a focus or just one.

Who needs to be present?

Just like a party, a meeting is not a meeting if there is nobody there! Meetings need participants, but not just *anyone*. We have already mentioned that the size of the meeting can have significant impact on the style, ambience, and how it is managed, and therefore another consideration has to be the number of people you wish to invite.

Some people actively avoid meetings and see them as time-wasters, whereas others almost seek them out – after all, a meeting is somewhere where you can speak out and be noticed (not to mention the free tea and biscuits). Therefore it is for you to consider whether you are encouraging some to attend or having to tactfully put others off.

Another consideration is whether they are the *right* people to attend. If you want real decisions to take place at your meeting, key decision makers (often those directly involved or who have a budget) must be present or no decision will be made. Let me demonstrate this through a scenario that happened to me, in the form of a case study.

Many years ago I was asked to take part in a meeting that aimed to bring together 13 different organizations to share a new training database. Using the shared database, any of the organizations who signed up to be a part of the programme could apply to go on any of the courses listed, thus making sure that the best use was made of the resources. It was a great idea and quite radical for its time. Let me share what actually happened.

At the first meeting all the key training managers were present, and the group worked towards agreeing a joint objective and terms of reference. The meeting was not well facilitated and there were no firm decisions, other than to come together again next month. Everyone left in a fairly positive spirit but with no real actions completed.

At the following meeting I noticed that three or four managers could not attend (due to commitments), but sent their deputies. This had a disastrous effect because they could not make a decision and had to take any outcomes back to their manager for consideration. Consequently the outcome was even less than last time and people left dissatisfied with the progress. I am sure you can guess what happened at the following meeting. Suddenly the attendees (if anyone attended at all) became the secretarial assistants, who could only take notes and did not even participate in the meeting! It is no surprise that the project broke down and the impetus was lost.

The message I took from this is that if you do not have influential key budget holders at your meeting, they will not be able to make the decisions and you are in danger of becoming a discussion group that can only debate issues – not act on them. Also, once your meeting has lost its momentum, it is very difficult to reignite it again. The lesson is clear:

Get it right first time and keep the motivation to attend high.

Let's go back to whom you need at your meeting. The simple reply to this is – everyone who is needed to make progress or can influence the outcome. Think wider than the original issue. Will any decision made in the meeting have an impact on others? If so, should *they* also be present?

Any guest speakers?

From time to time you may need to include guest speakers in the meeting. They may...

▶ ask to come along because they have information they feel is important
▶ be invited by the Chair to explain a situation/project or give information that is of use to the meeting members
▶ be invited to provide a diversion or variety in a meeting.

Whatever the reason, they need to be extended the same courtesy as any other guest. It is therefore useful to have someone from the meeting liaise with the guest to set the context, assure them of their relevance and acquaint them with necessary details such as:

▶ the time and date of the meeting
▶ the venue (including any parking or travel restrictions)
▶ whether there will be any presentation equipment available (should they wish to use slides or PowerPoint)
▶ whether they have handouts or documents that need circulating prior to the meeting
▶ the point at which they may access the room (some speakers like to set up beforehand, and this may not be possible)
▶ how long they will actually be presenting for (so that they may tailor their talk to match your time slot)
▶ your contact details in case they experience any problems with their journey
▶ what will happen afterwards (whether they join the meeting or are asked to leave).

Important point: Try to time your guest's slot as precisely as possible so that they are not left waiting outside the room. One way around this is to either ask your guest speaker to be the first item, so that they may then leave. Or allocate a time for their item so that it directly follows a break. If the meeting has then gone over time, you can either cancel the break (asking the meeting attendees to grab a drink and continue), or alternatively move the break until after your guest. Breaks are great for giving you 'catch up' time.

Try to ensure that someone is free to leave the meeting in order to escort your guest speaker out of the room or building, and thank them for their input and clarify any further actions (if necessary).

Collecting resources

Depending on the type of meeting you are holding, there may be a number of different resources that need to be pulled together:

PHYSICAL

▶ **Room** – unless you are using your office, you will need a meeting room. In some organizations you may need to book this in advance. An alternative is to book a meeting room in a nearby conference facility or hotel. Although this may be at a higher cost, it affords the benefit of neutrality – very important if the meeting includes negotiations.

TECHNICAL

▶ **Presentation** – are you going to need presentation equipment for either yourself or any of your other speakers? If so, you are possibly going to need a screen, projector and laptop, in case anyone only brings their presentation on a data stick.

GENERAL

▶ **Equipment** – for some meetings you may need to have certain equipment present such as samples or demonstration models. Where this is the case ensure you have the correct number of power sockets or extension cables to allow for a full demonstration – or space to allow for this.
▶ **Stationery** – depending on the nature of your meeting, you may need to lay out pens and paper for everyone, together with larger items needed in the room, such as a flip chart and board pens.

► **Paperwork** – bring additional copies of previous minutes and agendas in case they are needed, and also copies of any other accompanying notations, presentation material or paperwork.

Deciding on an outcome

Some meetings are more concerned with staff conversations and others are there to move business forward at a pace, in a structured way. I started this chapter by saying how important it is to have a purpose and focus for your meeting. It is also very important to have a solid **outcome**. Put it like this:

> **'For this meeting to be considered a success it must achieve...'**

– and then complete the sentence.

Do not concentrate on your wants – for example, 'For this meeting to be considered a success I *must* get allocated the project I want' is far too focused on your personal aims and desires. A meeting can still achieve its outcome even if individuals do not get what *they* want, but where a number of problems are solved.

Setting a firm outcome for the meeting – for example, 'For this meeting to be considered a success it must achieve a decided outcome for the project' – helps you to build a statement that now explicitly tells all attendees this.

For example:

> **'The main outcome of this meeting is to finally decide on whether the project will go forward and, if so, who will be responsible for its implementation.'**

This leaves all attendees in no doubt:

► as to the proposed subject of discussion
► that the Chair expects a solid result.

(In fact, in some meetings you are not allowed to leave until the outcome is met!)

Setting the agenda

Creating an agenda will enable everyone to know:

▶ **where the meeting is to be held** – usually an address line (don't forget to name the room if needed).

▶ **the time frame of the meeting** – always state the start time; however, whether you put a start *and* finish time on every item is reliant on style. Some agendas will put a finish time at the end of the agenda, especially if the room has to be vacated by a certain time.

▶ **possibly who is attending** – some agendas will state who is to attend, others do not. However, as most agendas are emailed out these days it is easy to see who else is invited. Some also put the name of the lead person beside each item that they wish to raise.

▶ **the name of the Chair** – this may provide additional weight to a staff member's decision to attend. It is also useful to name the Chair so that anyone entering the meeting on the day will automatically know their name.

▶ **a contact for any apologies or late items** – this may be the Chair or the name of an administrator. Not all agendas have this information but it can be particularly useful if someone is unable to attend.

▶ **the items to be discussed** – these usually form a numbered list and, although the agenda might even be reshuffled on the day, it is best practice that the Chair keeps to that order if at all possible, as not all attendees may attend for the full duration of the meeting and some may come later owing to the position of the item in the agenda.

▶ **anything the attendees need to bring** – if attendees are expected to bring anything with them, it is best if this is explicitly stated.

Tip

If you are sending attachments (such as corresponding papers for consideration or pre-reading), it is best to bring your readers' attention to this on the agenda, too.

Figures 3.1, 3.2 and 3.3 below are typical examples of informal, formal and business agendas respectively.

```
Team Meeting for the Recruitment Team
[date] – Lincoln Room, Darenth House, 2 p.m.
(Chair – Brenda Higgins)
                    AGENDA
1   Discussion regarding new IT system proposed for the coming year
2   Changes to employment legislation – an update
3   Impact of new legislation on current practice
    BREAK
4   Tim Hotley to provide a presentation on his streamlined system
5   The results of the Charity Dinner
6   Booking the Christmas meal
7   Any other business
```

Figure 3.1 An informal agenda for a team meeting.

```
                Kingsnorth Council Meeting
Notice is hereby given of the meeting of the Housing Committee
   To be held on [Date] at 7.30 p.m. at the Kingsnorth
                    Community Centre
             (Chair – Councillor Philip Long)
                    AGENDA
1   To receive Apologies for Absence and sign attendance register
2   To receive Declarations of Interest and lobbying
3   Minutes of the last meeting
4   Matters arising from the Minutes not otherwise on the agenda
5   Announcements from the Chair
6   Updates and items for authorization
7   To discuss the quotes received for repair work to the Homefield site
8   To discuss the contract for ABC Holdings
9   Permission sought for a new contractor for electrical requirements
10  Centre Manager requests a budget for the Christmas lights
11  Courses and Training
12  Financial matters
13  Future meeting schedules
14  Questions from Members of the Public and Councillors
```

Figure 3.2 A highly structured agenda for a council meeting.

Prodash Project Meeting
Meeting to be held: [date], at the PPR Offices, Wokingham
The Winslet Room, 15.00–17.00
(Chair for this meeting – Sylvia Holmes)

AGENDA

Attendees: Linda Salmon, Rosalind Mitchell, Kirsty Mullings, Jim Broyle, Pete Marcus, Lois Jennings (minute taker)

Administrator (for any additional items or apologies): Chris Mullins

Item number	Item	Time
1.	Introductions	15.00
2.	Overview of the work achieved so far	15.05
3.	Implementation of the new plan	15.20
4.	Signatories and first quarter payment details	16.00
5.	Future requests for funding	16.20
6.	Project summary document	16.35
7.	Action points collated	16.45
8.	Date of next meeting agreed	16.55
9.	END	17.00

Figure 3.3 A typical agenda for a project meeting (with timed entries).

KEEP IN MIND...

1 Always be clear on the purpose and/or focus of your meeting.

2 Ensure everyone knows what the meeting is about and who will be attending.

3 You need the influential players at your meeting, otherwise you will not create change.

4 Will your meeting have an impact on the work of others? Should they be invited, too?

5 Guest speakers can add additional interest to your meeting – just make sure they are fully briefed.

6 Always have spare pens and paper available for those who forget to bring them.

7 Test all technical equipment before the meeting to ensure it works.

8 If possible, load up everyone's presentation onto the laptop so that each speaker is ready to roll.

9 Don't be afraid to state the desired outcome. You may find it encourages a larger attendance as those invited may feel that it will trigger decisive action.

10 Your agenda is part of your marketing tool. It should be factual and contain all relevant information to ensure everyone understands what the meeting is for and how to attend.

4

....

Administration

In this chapter you will:
- **become familiar with the steps involved in administering a meeting**
- **consider how small details can affect a meeting**
- **learn how to create a smooth template for administering all future meetings.**

Calling a meeting

Meetings do not just happen – someone has to think through the issues and ensure that every aspect is considered. This could be a very important meeting where significant decisions are made and money changes hands. It is therefore essential that you take a measured and intelligent approach to creating the right atmosphere.

Whether you are calling the meeting yourself or have been asked by your manager to set up a meeting, you are now in the position of supporting the meeting throughout its duration.

Tip

If you are doing this for someone else, go back through the previous chapter and, using the headings as an aide-memoire, create a list to make sure that you have all the information you need.

The meeting may be either new or established.

If the meeting is a regular or established meeting, you will need to:

▶ look out the past minutes
▶ consider venue and time (Is it convenient for everyone to attend? Is there a pattern of certain people not attending?)

- ▶ if you decide to change the time or place of the meeting, highlight those changes so that everyone is aware of them
- ▶ check that you have agenda items from everyone.

If the meeting is totally **new,** you may need to:

- ▶ book a room
- ▶ ensure you have sufficient lead-in time for everyone to receive their invitation and confirm their attendance
- ▶ provide instructions as to how to find the venue and any parking or security protocols
- ▶ work with the Chair to establish who is to be invited (you may also need to discuss with the Chair the type of format they would prefer and any logos that need to be displayed on the paperwork)
- ▶ book or organize a minute taker (if necessary)
- ▶ create an agenda
- ▶ prepare a filing area (physical or electronic) where you will store all meeting notes for this and any future meetings.

If your meeting is a public meeting, then there may also be protocol surrounding the times that it can be called and the timescale – for example, you may need to advertise or have it announced in the local papers for weeks before the actual meeting, or you may need to hold it in the evening. If you are unsure as to whether your meeting falls into this category, it is best to ask.

Sending out invitations and paperwork

Even if everyone knows about the meeting, it is customary to draft a formal invitation to all attendees. The only time that this is not expected is when a meeting is regular – for example for a team meeting held every Monday morning.

If it is only a meeting request you may be able to send this out via your electronic calendar, and if the meeting is internal to your organization you may also be able to access other electronic diaries to ascertain whether people are likely to be free. However, bear in mind that not everyone keeps their diary up to date and, just because a date appears to be free, this does not mean that it definitely is.

So many people use email now that this will probably be your chosen method of contacting everyone. However, if you are inviting people from outside of your own organization, you cannot assume that they have an email account or that they read their messages frequently. Some people may read their emails only periodically and might miss your invitation.

Tip

Do not fall into the trap of assuming that because you have sent an invitation, it has arrived safely, and has been read by the correct person. Many emails and letters go missing en route, or they may be opened by someone else. Always ask for confirmation of receipt and attendance.

Your invitation may also require further information or documents to be attached. If this is so, make certain that you have not only attached the documents but also that you refer to them in the body of the invitation so that it brings the reader's attention to the fact that they are there. A possible invitation (by letter) may look like this:

Subject: ABC Project Meeting – [date]

Dear [name]

I would like to invite you to a meeting to discuss the commencement of the ABC Project. The meeting is scheduled for 14.30 on [date] at [place].

To prepare for the meeting, I have attached the original specification for the project. Although things have undoubtedly moved on since this was first written, it would be helpful if you could read through the original specification as a starting point. I can then outline the changes and update everyone from there.

It would be helpful for numbers and catering if you could <u>confirm your attendance</u>, but in the first instance please could you <u>confirm by return mail</u> that you have received this invitation and the attachments.

Many thanks,

Mandy Middleton

Project Leader

Figure 4.1 Sample invitation to a meeting.

Creating the right environment

Creating the right environment for the meeting can help matters move more freely and set the tone of the meeting. At a basic level, think of a more formal set-up for a formal meeting and an informal set-up for an informal meeting:

Formal meeting	Informal meeting
Chairs around or across a table	Possibly just a ring of chairs or even people sitting at their desks or workstations
It is important that everyone is seated where they can see each other	In a crushed area, some people may have a restricted view
Paperwork set out neatly for reference	May not know in advance what paperwork is needed
Cables and connections may be needed for laptops	Laptops not always needed
To enhance concentration the room should be plainly decorated and not have too many distractions	You may prefer a room with more 'personality' or colour
For long, tense meetings, water and air conditioning may be needed	Drinks can be ad hoc and meeting many not be quite so tense or long and protracted

Let's look at some of these factors in more detail:

▶ **Room size** – how many people are coming to the meeting? The room needs to be large enough to seat everyone comfortably, but not so large that you feel that you are filling only a small area. If the room is too small, it becomes difficult to concentrate and the temperature in the room will rise rapidly through body heat. A very large room might seem a better solution but again it is not ideal as the space around you may not feel very comfortable or relaxed.

▶ **Furnishings** – unless they are very informal, most meetings require some form of table and seating arrangement. For a small meeting, this may be a coffee table; for a larger meeting, a boardroom table and, in a council situation, possibly the council chamber itself. Most Chairs prefer a round or oval table, if possible. This is because attendees tend to get lost in the corners of oblong tables and it is more difficult to see them. Also, rounder tables give the impression of equality, as opposed to someone sitting at the 'head' of the table. Pay close attention to seating, too – the attendees may be sitting in them for some time, and therefore the chairs need to be as comfortable and supportive as possible.

▶ **Decor** – the more neutral the room, the easier it will be to think. Fancy decor distracts and, if there are, say, the remains of someone's leaving party in the room, make sure everything is removed. Some attendees may be from other organizations and you want to give as professional an image as possible.

▶ **Temperature** – it should be possible to alter the temperature in the room through either a heating or cooling mechanism. Overly warm rooms will have a soporific effect on the meeting and less may be achieved. Overly cool and the attendees will not be able to concentrate and may refuse to remove their coats, creating a difficult start to the meeting.

▶ **Refreshments** – unless the meeting is very short, it is traditional to offer tea and coffee at the start of the meeting and have water available throughout the duration. If the meeting goes on for several hours, a mid-meeting tea/coffee break may also be included. The provision of biscuits and other refreshments will vary from company to company, and there may be strict rules about the provision of these – therefore check out what is acceptable.

▶ **Technical facilities** – if everyone brings laptops into the meeting (as is increasingly becoming the norm), they may need power cables and Internet access (unless access is possible through

Wi-Fi). Additionally, a screen and projector may need to be set up for presentations. Not all rooms are able to support this, and therefore checking the room against needs is essential.

▶ **Plants** – there is no doubt that plants bring a certain informality and relaxation to a room. They can soften a harsh environment and introduce a more relaxed atmosphere to even the starkest of rooms. However, be guided by your own environment and do not drag the entire company plant collection into the room with you!

▶ **Lighting** – I personally do not like rooms with no windows or, conversely, complete 'goldfish bowl' rooms with glass walls where there is lots of light and everyone can see in. The first I find too restrictive and the second too invasive. Ideally, natural lighting is best in any room but, where that is not possible, try to achieve a lighting effect that is as near to natural lighting as possible. Both glaringly bright lights and subtle 'ambience' lighting can cause headaches and eye strain, problems with reading computer screens and projections, and may interfere with everyone's train of thought.

> **Insight**
> You may think that where you hold a negotiating meeting does not really matter but both parties may suggest holding it on their own premises. This is because the 'home team' has an advantage this way (similar to sport). To avoid this, negotiation meetings are best held on neutral territory.

Considering details of courtesy

Many meetings will involve only internal staff and naturally you would be courteous to them, but on occasions you may be organizing meetings where the attendees come from other companies or organizations. When this happens it is essential that you offer them every courtesy so that they also form a good impression of your company. It is not simply customer care but showing deep consideration – and it is noticed by everyone, not just the guests.

Let's go through some of the key courtesy points. There may be other considerations you wish to employ in your own organization, but these are the basics:

► **Venue details** – if your attendee or guest has not been to the venue before, it would be helpful to send them a map (including the full address details of the venue). Most venues have these already and therefore you can simply ask them to send you a map electronically. On the details they will usually also have the venue phone number, but it might also be helpful to send through your own mobile number, just in case the guest gets stuck in traffic, takes a wrong turn, or looks like being exceptionally late.

► **Special needs** – this covers two areas. The first concerns special needs in terms of dietary refreshments – for example, gluten-free biscuits and soya milk are now widely available. The second area concerns disability. Do any of your guests need wheelchair access? A hearing loop? Someone to sign for them? A carer to be present? All of these can be made available if you enquire in advance; trying to organize this at the last minute would be very difficult indeed.

► **Booking a parking space** – this very much depends on your company's or organization's policy. Some organizations may have spaces that are reserved for visitors. If you know that your guests are travelling to you by car, and you are able to reserve a space, it makes a wonderful gesture to organize this for them (you will also know that they will not have to waste time driving around looking for somewhere to park their car, and that may be some distance away).

► **Greeting at reception** – if you are able, on the day of the meeting, inform your reception staff of your guest's name and how they should be greeted (including whether they should be sent up to the room or wait in reception for you to come and escort them to the meeting). Being greeted politely by reception staff and appearing to be expected provides a warm and welcoming impression of a very professional organization.

► **Arranging for a pass/badge** – as security is important in many organizations, it is highly possible that your guests will need to be issued with a name badge and possibly a card or key that allows electronic entry through the internal doors within the building. These usually have to be signed for and handed back at the end of the day. All guests usually also need to sign a visitors' log, as you are responsible for them in case of a fire.

- ▶ **Escorted to the room** – as mentioned above, you may decide to meet your guest in reception and then escort them personally to the room. This has a number of advantages in that you can make sure all of the registration details are completed, and you can begin to build rapport as you escort them to the room by asking them questions about their journey.
- ▶ **Toilets and other facilities** – if they have made a long journey or plan to be in the meeting for some time, your guests may need to use the bathroom or kitchen facilities. It is helpful to direct their attention to these prior to the meeting so that they know where they are, when needed.
- ▶ **Welcome presentation** – it is becoming increasingly popular to start off any meeting where guests are present with not only a personal welcome but also a run-through of any health and safety issues (such as fire alarms, emergency evacuation procedures and location of muster points), as well as of any organizational policies on the use of camera phones and laptops and so on.

Insight

Best practice is that, if you are responsible for the administration of a meeting, even if you are not taking part in the meeting itself, you should remain on the premises in case you are needed at any time during the meeting or if it ends early. However, this is not always possible, so it is best to discuss the situation with the Chair.

Following the meeting

You may or may not be present throughout the entire meeting but there are actions to be taken following the meeting.

Immediately following the meeting you may need to escort any guests or visitors out of the building, handing in badges, security cards and possibly signing them out of the visitors' log book. You may also need to just check that they know how to:

- ▶ exit from the car park or parking lot
- ▶ deal with any additional security barriers
- ▶ exit the business park
- ▶ return to their main route home.

Some visitors will come by public transport and they may need you to either point them in the direction of a bus stop or nearby railway station. They may also need you to call a taxi cab.

With your visitors or guests safely on their way, return to the room
to clean up any residue left by the meeting, such as handouts, pens
and drinks. Most organizations have a policy that a room should be
left clean and clear for the next person.

When you return to your desk, you will need to contact the Chair as
soon as possible (if you did not actually attend the meeting) to find
out if there were any presentations given or additional information
handed out. This is so that you can send a message out to everyone
who attended the meeting to:

▶ thank them for attending
▶ ask them to send you any copies of presentation material used
  during the meeting (or any promised attachments to go out with
  the minutes)
▶ and possibly mention the date of the next meeting or provide, in
  shortened form, a summary of the next steps.

Two examples are shown below in Figures 4.2 and 4.3 – the first is
a general thank you while the second is aimed at a particular guest.

Dear All,

Thank you for your attendance today at the PAD project meeting.
If you provided any presentation material during the meeting or
have any attachments you would like to circulate, please send
them to me by Friday 25 April as I will be sending out the minutes
on Monday.

As a quick reminder for your diaries, the next PAD project
meeting will take place on 30 May in the same venue.

Many thanks,

Pat Glen

PAD Project Administrator

Figure 4.2 General text for all meeting attendees.

Dear Stephanie,

Thank you for your attendance today at the PAD project meeting – your input was greatly appreciated. Please could you send me a copy of the presentation material you used together with any other information you promised the team by Friday 25 April as I will be sending out the minutes on Monday 28th and would like to include them.

If you need any more information or would like to discuss any aspect of the meeting, please ring me on [telephone number].

Many thanks,

Pat Glen

PAD Project Administrator

Figure 4.3 Possible text for a particular guest.

Distributing the notes

The construction of minutes is dealt with in detail in Part four and therefore I will only mention the distribution of notes here. The notes must go out as soon as possible. The reason for this is that everyone must have a chance of reading them and taking action on any of the highlighted actions required. If the meeting is monthly, this really means making sure that the minutes in note form are out within the first week following the meeting. If it is a weekly meeting, they need to be distributed either the same day as the meeting or the one following it.

Sitting on notes and minutes is very poor practice. I have been at some meetings where the first item is handing out the minutes from the last meeting. When this happens, my heart sinks. Unless the attendees made their own notes, it is very unlikely that any actions will have occurred and valuable meeting time is also lost while everyone reads and debates the contents. This type of organization can clog up the system of meetings and make it extremely difficult to work productively.

Tip

If you are distributing minutes by email, put a tracer on them so that you know who has opened the document. It will not prove that the recipient has actually read the contents, but one of the most frequent excuses given by those who have not made progress on their actions is that they did not receive the minutes. This then falls as a criticism aimed at the administrator. If you have put a tracer on the email, you can at least point out that the file was received and opened. (The postal equivalent of this is sending by recorded delivery where at least someone has to sign to verify that the letter arrived at its destination.)

KEEP IN MIND...

1 Create an easy aide-memoire, or checklist, to help you organize meetings quickly and effectively.

2 Check for any protocols regarding the meeting set-up.

3 Allow plenty of time for people to receive your information and respond. Do not assume everyone has email or is comfortable using it.

4 Do not accidentally give out everyone's email address.

5 If you are responsible for booking a meeting into a room, go and visit it first to assess whether it is suitable.

6 Liaise with the Chair as to how they would like the room set up and whether refreshments are needed and when.

7 Being courteous is not just about customer care; it also gives a good impression of the company to any guests.

8 It is never too early to start building rapport.

9 Thank everyone for attending the meeting and ask for any paperwork or slides that need circulating.

10 Distribute the minutes plus any documents as soon as possible to allow everyone to start on their actions.

Part two

Participation in meetings

5

Pre-planning

In this chapter you will:
* *consider what aspects of pre-planning are necessary*
* *appreciate the importance of revisiting the minutes*
* *consider whether to address the Chair prior to the meeting.*

Registering your acceptance

As an attendee at a meeting you have a responsibility to come to the meeting fully prepared. If you do not prepare, it is likely that you will not be able to participate as fully as is necessary. You were invited because your specific area of expertise or business is involved and valued in the decision and therefore to come ill-prepared is to appear not interested.

Let us first consider the investment made in inviting staff to attend a meeting. In the world of business, time is money. Therefore meetings that are productive are a great time-saver (and make good financial sense). Have you ever thought how much it costs to stage a meeting? Or how much it costs for you to attend a meeting? It is good to do this, so try out the following simple calculation:

> Try this
> If you have a daily rate, the maths is simple – divide your daily rate by the number of hours you work in the day. For example:
> **£100** per day works out at **£12.50** per hour for working an eight-hour day.

If you don't have a daily rate:
1 Take your annual salary – say £**18,000**.
2 Divide by **233** (for the number of saleable consultancy days you could sell a year*) – this will give you your daily rate.
3 Then calculate your hourly rate as above.

For example:
a salary of £**18,000** would give you a per hour rate of approximately £**9.66**.

*When calculating the number of days in a year you need to deduct **104** days for weekends, eight bank holidays, and **20** days of annual leave, as these are generally non-earning days.

That is simply for your salary. Now multiply that figure for the number of people around the table and you will get a very approximate cost of running that meeting for one hour. (Obviously some people will be paid more than you and others less, but it is a good rule of thumb.) For a two-hour meeting, double this figure, and so on.

This amount does not include the price of any refreshments or room hire. You can now see that the meeting costs are stacking up and it is becoming increasingly important that the meeting has a valuable outcome to warrant such company expenditure. To ensure the value is exploited to the full, you need to come to the meeting prepared, having done some initial pre-planning in terms of practical actions and thinking.

Previously I discussed how to send out an invitation to a meeting. Now you are on the receiving end of this invitation. Unless the meeting is a casual one (or a public meeting where anyone can drift into the room), you will need to return a formal acceptance. Acceptance is needed to enable the administrator to…

▶ **ensure the room is of the correct size** – remember cost and comfort – you won't want to be squashed into a tiny room and a very large room may be unnecessary.
▶ **confirm the catering arrangements** (if necessary) – too little and the administrator may feel embarrassed when they run out of drinks after the first five cups (especially if there are guests). Too much and the administrator may waste food that might go uneaten… and that represents a cost to the project.

- ▶ **confirm to the Chair that representatives are present** – if representatives from other organizations or projects are required, the administrator will need to confirm with the Chair which ones will be attending the meeting. If just one key organization is missing, it may be that decisions cannot be made.
- ▶ **speak with the Chair about who is attending for each aspect of the meeting** – the Chair may have decided that someone from the Communications Department needs to be present to hear and respond to that aspect of the project. For example, my manager asks me to attend because I work in the Communications Department, but I usually write press releases, and perhaps the Chair, when thinking of 'communications', actually wanted someone who could run some quick refresher workshops on writing reports. It may have been better to have invited someone from the Training Department instead. If the administrator knows who is attending, they can correct the mistake before it becomes a waste of time for everyone.
- ▶ **create name badges or attendance lists** – unless the administrator knows who is attending they are unable to create name badges or a signing-in or attendance sheet. They would also be unable to send out any pre-reading required in advance of the meeting. Some computer programs will generate badges or attendance lists automatically, and these can then be sent out with any papers, or emailed.
- ▶ **inform reception regarding visitors and parking** – a list of attendees can be left with reception which means that you will be met in an organized manner (and possibly allocated a reserved car park space if you need it).
- ▶ **correct any name spellings** – many names are not spelled in the way that they are pronounced. Names are intensely personal and to get it wrong can cause gross embarrassment. By registering your attendance, the meeting organizers can check your name to avoid any slip-ups on the day.

It is therefore not just good manners to formally accept an invitation to a meeting but in doing so you are also being very helpful in the process of organizing that meeting.

One final point – if you accept, but just before the meeting find out that you cannot go, check whether it is acceptable to send a colleague in your place. Apart from the fact that it is courteous to inform people when such changes are made, the Chair may prefer to reorganize the entire meeting for another date, rather than have you not attend. In other words, your input may be so important that no decisions can be made without you present.

Checking the details

As part of pre-planning you need to check all the details and enter them into your diary, personal organizer or scheduler. It is very easy (particularly with some of the automatic diary systems) to forget to enter where the meeting is to take place, and at what time.

Being late because you are stuck in traffic is acceptable; being late because you went to the wrong venue is not. The first is beyond your control but the second is completely within your control and this makes you look highly disorganized.

Also, do not assume that, because a meeting has been in Room 12 for the past four months, that it will be in Room 12 *this* month. Venues do change and switch based on their availability and whether a different room is needed on this occasion. The same is true of time. The meeting may have been held at 2 p.m. for the past few weeks but it may not continue to be so.

It is only when you check over the details that you find out you will need to reserve a parking space in advance if you need one, or that you will need to read the attachment sent through last month because you will be asked to comment on it. So many people fail to carry out what the invitation has asked them to do and turn up unprepared. If you remember the point I made in Chapter 1 regarding where you are most likely to meet influential or senior people – in a meeting – you'll see how turning up ill-prepared gives a very poor impression. Five minutes of checking the information in advance can allow you time to prepare fully so that you make a great impression on others present.

> **Tip**
> A few minutes checking details can make the difference between getting to the meeting on time or sitting in an empty room, wondering where everyone is.

Finally, spend a little time making some short notes on the meeting. First, look at the title of the meeting and the agenda (if that is available at this time). What role will you be taking in this meeting? Are you there to defend an issue or promote something? Are you the link with another department or even another organization? What is your company's stance on the situation?

Case study

Imagine you work for a fashion magazine and you have been asked to a meeting to view a top designer's new seasonal range in which he has included a lot of jackets with real fur collars and cuffs. Irrespective of your own feelings and views, what stance would your magazine take?

Would you be promoting it? After all, he is famous and it is the latest style. Surely the designer would have to carry any backlash from anti-fur protestors, wouldn't he?

Should you refuse? Your magazine has banned any clothing that uses real fur; in fact, you have had several features on this issue over the past few years. OK, he is a famous designer but your readers are important and they trust you – anyway you could still feature him by doing another feature on anti-fur but using him as an example.

Can you find a 'halfway house'? Should you be suggesting that you would like to see his non-fur items only, even if that means just skirts and trousers – not the full outfits? The designer may be offended but he is still getting some publicity.

Unless you had thought through this situation prior to the meeting, it would be easy to find yourself on the back foot in the meeting and unable to make a decision there and then or, worse still, making the decision based on your feelings – not the company's stance. Any decision you make in a hurry would also carry with it worry about whether it was the 'right' decision. It is far better to think through and research your stance before getting anywhere near the meeting.

Make notes of what the issues are, where there could be negotiation, and any other aspects that you feel might be useful in the meeting.

Consulting with other parties

There is a possibility that you are attending the meeting as a spokesperson, perhaps for your own project team or a stakeholder organization. If so, you will need to consult with your own team/organization before you go to the meeting. We have all laughed about meetings needing pre-meetings but the truth is that, if you are attending a meeting as a representative of someone else or your entire project team who are waiting back at base, you need to liaise with all of them before the meeting and find out their views and any points they may want you to raise.

In some instances there may also need to be some research to be undertaken before the meeting. If this is the case, then you will need to meet with the researchers to ensure you thoroughly understand the issues around the research questions, the sample details and how the results have been calculated.

Tip

Where the research is complex or the outcome controversial, it is possibly worth a research assistant attending the meeting with you, just in case there are questions you cannot answer.

Depending on the nature of the meeting, you may also decide that you need a strategy. If, for example, the meeting is to decide on how three project teams will work together, your own project team may have some strong feelings about that subject! You are really taking part in a form of *negotiation* and there will probably be the need to make concessions. These need to be agreed with the team *before* you enter the meeting, so that you know what bargaining power you have when you are thrust into the centre of negotiations.

What you need to take to the meeting

Hopefully you now also have a page or two of personal notes as well as any papers and attachments to take in with you. Most people who attend lots of meetings record meeting information in a day book. This is simply an A4-sized, fully lined, hard-backed notebook. Using it means that all meeting notes are maintained in one place. At the top of the page write the date and time, the name of the meeting and who was present. You can then complete it with your thoughts and notes to refer back to later. (If decisions were made at the meeting that affect your area of business, you may also need to compare the minutes with your notes.)

Insight

If you want to be completely electronic and take a laptop, tablet or netbook into the meeting to make your notes, be aware that this is not always acceptable. Check with the Chair as a matter of courtesy as electronic devices can be annoying to others in the meeting. If you are going to use an electronic device, make sure that you carry a mains cable or have enough power in your laptop to last the meeting. You may find yourself in a room without mains power sockets and out of power. This may make you feel disorganized, as you will have to ask to borrow a pen and paper.

Naturally you will need to take any pre-reading attachments and also the previous minutes and a copy of the agenda, but you may also need to take other items with you – perhaps some speculative work that you need to show, a piece of equipment, or anything that illustrates your point.

As you will also be taking *yourself*, I think it pertinent to mention the clothes that you will be wearing. Your clothes need to be comfortable but they also need to represent both your company and also the seriousness of your role or position. For example, in the legal profession black is favoured or charcoal-grey suits and white shirts. In another company they may require staff to wear navy blue (representing the company livery), but within that range your role or position may dictate the use of coloured tops or blouses/shirts. Some meetings are very informal and in an IT company you may find that dressing in jeans and a T-shirt is more appropriate. Dressing appropriately will enable you to feel comfortable and assertive enough to challenge any issue that you find unacceptable.

Finally, take a small bottle of water or a fruit drink carton with you. Meetings can be long – if you speak regularly your throat may become dry, and catering is not always supplied.

Past minutes and actions

Sometimes it seems like there is no time to even think about past minutes; you rush out of the meeting thinking you'll deal with them later when they come through. But then you don't notice when the email arrives and you forget about the meeting the following week because something else comes up. Sound familiar? If so, you are in fire-fighting mode and it may even be that you see the email with the minutes come through but you blank it. It hardly needs saying that this is not a good way of organizing your time or running a business.

Later in this book I will tackle minute taking in detail and there I am explicit about the timescale within which minutes should be distributed. (If this is not happening in your organization, copy that page of this book and hand it round to your minute-taking staff.) You can do this as a gift from me because I believe speed in minute distribution is so important to the whole meeting process.

In future, when you see a set of minutes in your in-box or arrive in the post, grab them with enthusiasm and first scan the action column or area. Is your name there? If so, use a highlighter pen to highlight your name (some administrators do this for you to bring your attention to your own required actions). Now go back to the beginning and quickly scan the text, all the while asking yourself: 'Is this a reasonable representation of the meeting?' Don't get hung up on grammar or start thinking, 'I wouldn't have written it like this' – instead, concentrate on the content.

After you have scanned the whole document, go back to the sections that include actions for you. Read them through again. Are they clear? Is the action correct? If not, you need to contact the Chair and/or the project manager immediately for clarification. If it is clear and correct, locate your diary or scheduler, and mark out a period of time when you will undertake the tasks required of you.

This whole process should take no longer than it would to make a cup of decent tea. Once the job is done, you can file the minutes away in your regular place, feeling confident that you also have time allocated in your diary to complete your tasks.

Tip

The largest time-waster in business is procrastination – thinking and worrying about something can take longer than the actual task. Just get on and do it!

Addressing the Chair prior to the meeting

You may need to speak to the Chair prior to the meeting. This could be for a number of reasons including:

▶ to explain a disability or personal injury
▶ to provide some background information
▶ to introduce yourself
▶ to clarify that you are the correct person to be present at the meeting
▶ to familiarize yourself with the project and its outcomes

...to name but a few.

However, contact the Chair *only* if you have something to discuss that is relevant to the meeting or affects it in some way. Most Chairs are more than keen to discuss any issue that will make the meeting flow better or increase the possibility of a decision being made – in other words, anything that simplifies or speeds up the process. Lobbying for support on any issue is usually less welcome; therefore tread with care if that is your intention.

KEEP IN MIND...

1 Calculate the value of your time – that is the investment the company has in you attending a meeting.

2 Preparation is not just being organized with pens and paper; it also includes thinking.

3 Always confirm your attendance. It is not just about being polite; it actually helps others to organize the meeting.

4 If you plan to send someone else in your place, inform the Chair or meeting administrator.

5 Wear smart clothes that are representative of your business – they will aid you to feel more confident and you will be taken more seriously.

6 Liaise with all relevant parties before the meeting to gather their views.

7 If you know you are not good at processing minutes, create a process that works fast.

8 Book time out to tackle your actions – you will feel so much more in control.

9 Try to complete your actions before the following meeting.

10 It is fine to contact the Chair prior to a meeting as long as the issue is about the meeting.

6

Being a speaker

In this chapter you will:
- *think about the opportunities you have to speak out in meetings*
- *learn how to structure a short talk*
- *consider strategies for handling questions.*

Why might you be called to be a speaker?

Being asked to speak or present in a meeting is a mixed blessing. On the one hand, you are thrust into the limelight and you have a great opportunity to glow. On the other, you might expose your lack of skills in what can be – many people would agree – a very tricky area.

The great thing about giving a talk in a meeting is that, unlike an interview, the subject matter is not likely to be *you*. The most common scenario is that, as part of your presentation, you are presenting data and/or ideas for the group's consideration. Therefore it is less about you and more about the subject matter – phew!

There are other positive factors:

▶ **They might be people you know** – in an internal meeting, it is highly likely that your audience will be people you actually know, in which case you can be less formal and the entire presentation can be like a chat between friends. You might not even have to stand up; you may present the whole agenda item sitting down, in your regular seat.
▶ **There is less pressure to perform** – the people around the table or in the room are not there to judge you. They are not going to grab a grid and give you marks out of ten for your performance!

If anything, they are more likely to be far more focused on the actual information (and what it means to their project) than your style of delivery.

You should know more than your audience on this one – so let's look at the information. You are probably presenting a product or some data linked to a project or piece of work that you (or your team) have undertaken. This means that you will automatically know more about the subject than anyone else in front of you. For once, you will be the expert and so it is less likely that anyone will trip you up with a tricky question.

The main reason for being asked to speak in a meeting is that it is felt you have a project or information that is important for all to hear about. It might be that you have undertaken a particularly interesting piece of work or research, or maybe that you have some data for consideration.

If you have been asked to come in and speak to a team from another company (in other words, you are a guest speaker), it could be that same research again, or it may be that you have a product you wish to promote.

Sales staff are quite proficient at their job, so let's leave them to sell in the way they have been taught and concentrate on the scenario that you have just completed a piece of research you were undertaking as part of a qualification and your findings have interested a wide variety of people. Naturally they would love you to come in and speak about it. Let's imagine that your study found that being positive at work leads to greater job satisfaction. That might be useful to a whole host of companies and their HR departments. You may be asked to speak to staff welfare groups, the personnel and training departments, and possibly even the board. Each of these groups of people will be considering the implications of the research from their own perspective, and, as a guest in this situation, you may never know the impact that your research might have on changing the policies and practices of each organization. Powerful stuff!

Another reason you may be invited in to speak is to familiarize the meeting members with your work. Let's look at a case study to explore this idea.

Imagine that a new computer project is being set up to pull together all the computerized training systems within a council. There are three systems in this scenario and at the present time the computer project team does not know whether it will go with one of the three current systems, and integrate it throughout, or whether a new system needs to be built that takes the best from each of the three current ones.

To get the project off to a flying start, the project team needs to know what the current systems are, how they work and the benefits of each. The project team could go to all three venues but it makes more sense, at the familiarization stage, to ask a member of staff from each of the three training teams to come to a meeting and give an overview of their system and how it supports their work. This is a much better use of time because the project team can all sit in one room and learn in a morning what might otherwise have taken them three separate visits – possibly equating to three days out of the office.

In this scenario you would probably be allocated around 30 minutes to present the points asked of you. You may not be the manager; in fact, in this scenario the manager may not be the person best placed to give this information. Far better is a member of staff who uses the computer program regularly and understands all its nuances. They will be more able to comment on the program as a working tool, and therefore be more helpful to the project team.

Therefore anyone can be called to be a speaker at any time, and so let's look at the aspects you need to consider to ensure the situation goes smoothly.

What to assume and what *not* to assume

In essence, it is best not to assume anything and check everything! I was asked to speak at a conference many years ago where I assumed that, because I was invited to speak about a recent project I had undertaken, my audience wanted to know the results. I decided to create a full and interesting talk that would really make them think.

I was somewhat deflated to find out when I arrived part way through the conference that I was booked as a 'filler' because another speaker had backed out, that the audience were all teaching staff and would probably have no interest in my project other than being polite – oh and could I cut the talk down to ten minutes because the other speakers had wildly overrun!

I learned that day *never* to assume anything – including who the audience is and what they might want out of the talk.

So how can you make sure that you learn from my mistake and not repeat it? The key to this is asking some pertinent questions before agreeing to speak. If you are able, as soon as someone asks you to speak at a meeting, get in contact with the Chair. This can be in person or by email and reply in a way similar to this...

I have just been informed by my manager that you would like me to present the findings from my project at a future meeting. As I am sure you are aware, the project covered many aspects and I want to make sure that the people at the meeting receive the information that would be most interesting to them, and benefit their work. Therefore can I ask:

- ▶ What group of people will I be talking to?
- ▶ What is the level of seniority?
- ▶ What is the purpose of including this project – is there a particular section of the project that you think would interest them most?
- ▶ Would you like me to factor in time for questions?
- ▶ Will this talk be one in a series of talks or is it part of a usual meeting?
- ▶ What time would you like me to speak?
- ▶ How long would you like me to speak for?
- ▶ Do you have someone I could liaise with regarding equipment and facilities?

I am sorry there are so many questions but I want to make sure that my talk is targeted to the group and that they gain most benefit from it.

Regards,

Paul Lincoln.

Figure 6.1 Sample email/letter from a potential guest speaker to the Chair, asking for clarification.

Once the Chair has been back to you with the answers to these questions, you can move onto the person they have recommended as liaison. For example...

Dear John

I have been asked by the Chair of the TTM Project Group to come to their next meeting and present the findings of my recent study. I have been scheduled to speak at 11 a.m. on the agenda and would like some assistance in organizing my equipment in advance of this. In the first instance can I ask:

► Will there be a laptop, projector and screen in the room? (If not, are there sockets for running an extension lead to my own equipment?)
► Can the lighting be controlled or curtains closed?
► Is there a photocopying facility on the premises?
► Can I gain access to the room to set up or familiarize myself with the equipment before the meeting begins?
► Could you possibly provide me with a mobile phone number for a contact on the day?

Many thanks for your help,

Paul Lincoln.

Figure 6.2 Sample email/letter from guest speaker to the person organizing the meeting.

By making no assumptions and checking everything *before* even beginning to structure my talk, I now...

► have access to a load of useful information that will help me construct my talk
► can calm my nerves regarding the set-up
► have made contact with the Chair and organizer of the group, thereby breaking down initial barriers
► in a roundabout way have confirmed that I am expected on that day, at that time.

Tip

Always enquire whether you are the only speaker, and, if there are others, ask for their details so that you can liaise in respect of content. There is nothing worse than repeating points and using examples that have been used by a speaker before you.

Now we are ready to structure our talk in a way that really helps those listening.

Structuring your talk

It is crucial to find out two key pieces of information before you even begin to structure your talk. First, you need to know where your audience will be coming from; and second, the length of time you have available. The answer to the former will dictate your content and the answer to the latter will dictate the design and structural outline avoid one-word line.

THE AUDIENCE

I alluded to this in the previous section, but let's now split this into three sections.

1 The focus of the material
Yes, you could attend the meeting and talk about *your* project and what *you* found interesting about it – but this may not be of interest to your audience. Of course they will be polite, nod sagely all the way through and then politely thank you at the end – but they will also either forget you five minutes later or talk among themselves as to why you had been invited. Far better to centre the talk on what *they* want to know and how your project could help *them*. Hopefully you will have this information if you have already contacted the Chair, but, if not, you must ask it specifically:

▶ 'What would you like to gain from my input to your meeting?'
▶ 'Which specific part of my project would you like me to feature and why?'
▶ 'How do you see my project interrelating with the business of those at the meeting?'
▶ 'I want to make sure that I give your staff the most important messages from my research – do you know what would be most interesting and useful for everyone to hear?'

2 What do people already know?
If the audience already have a working knowledge of your project, or it has already been wildly promoted through the organizational newsletter, skim very quickly over the background. There are

occasions when you do need to assume some level of background knowledge to avoid wasting valuable speaking time and/or boring your audience to death by repeating what they have heard several times before. One way around this is to provide a short handout on the background to the project for those who want and need to know this detail.

3 What level are the audience?

It can be helpful to find out the organizational level of your audience. This will also help you to integrate relevant examples into your talk. It is no use speaking to senior managers and relating an example pertaining to an administrative role, in the same way as it would be unhelpful to expect a group of administration staff to find examples of setting strategy useful to them.

THE LENGTH OF TIME

Learn to talk to time. If you have been allotted 15 minutes, speak for 15 minutes (or ten minutes and allow five minutes for questions – whatever is appropriate). It is rude and unprofessional to overrun.

The remainder of your structure will follow a basic format:

▶ *Beginning/introduction* – introduce yourself, the project and its aims.
▶ *Middle section 1* – explain the project further (if necessary), then focus on the particular section that your audience needs. Refer to any background handouts and discuss the data (your findings).
▶ *Middle section 2 (optional)* – explain how your findings may help their business. This can be through examples, case studies, or a question-and-answer session.
▶ *Conclusion* – the conclusion of your project. (Leave the audience with any salient points or key facts you want them to remember.)
▶ *Questions (optional)* – you may decide to hold an open question-and-answer session at the end.

If your speaking time is 15 minutes, as mentioned earlier, then you are looking at a possible format of:

Time	Section	Points to cover	Slides/handouts
11.00	Introduction	My intro Aims of the project Questions at the end	1 – my intro 2 – project aims
11.03	M section 1	Why the project? Who was involved? What did we find?	Handout 3 – who was involved 4 – general findings
11.07	M section 2	Points that may be interesting to this group	5 – specific findings for this group
11.12	Conclusion/ questions	Final conclusion	6 – final message
11.15	End		7 – end slide

When using a presentation program such as PowerPoint, as a rule of thumb, you should allow three minutes for each slide at the most (and then add a header and end slide). A 15-minute talk would therefore need approximately:

15 divided by 3 = 5 slides plus 2 (header and end slide) = 7 slides

Keep slide information to main bullet points and speak around each point (if you have three bullet points on each of your main slides, that only gives you one minute of explanation on each point).

Insight

Naturally you do not need to always prepare a slide presentation for your talk – you can just speak – but having a structured plan is still useful as it shows you whether it is possible to achieve what you want in the time available.

Taking additional information with you

As you can see in the previous section, although you may have been initially daunted by giving a 15-minute presentation, when you start to plan it out, 15 minutes really isn't very long – perhaps not even long enough for you to convey everything you hoped. There is a possibility that you could negotiate with the Chair for a longer time slot, but this would extend their meeting and this may not be acceptable. If this is the case, then you need to find some way of providing a proportion of your information in a different format.

The key question you need to ask yourself when preparing or distributing documents is whether you intend them to...

▶ provide new and additional information only (background, items that you did not have time to include)
▶ reinforce your presentation (remind everyone of the salient points)
▶ provide a mixture of both.

The objective you choose will dictate how and what material you present, and how you manage the interface between the documents and your presentation.

I have already mentioned handouts, and these can be ideal. You may already have some leaflets produced for the project but they will be impersonal and not necessarily geared specifically to this group.

Create a handout containing a short background to the project (if necessary), the points you wish to make, and (possibly) a copy of your slide presentation. Make sure that any handout you give has the project name displayed together with your name and contact details, and, at the end of your talk, mention that if anyone would like to speak further, your details are on the handout.

Tip

Handouts do not have to be given in paper format. They can be presented electronically on a disk (perhaps even including a promotional film) or on a data stick. Using materials like these can also give you the opportunity of displaying your contact details.

Handling questions

If you have given a relevant and interesting presentation, it is highly likely that people will want to ask you questions. The main problem with questions is that they can run on, and it is too late if you have allocated three minutes for questions and then a dozen hands go up. You are trapped.

If you are going to do a lengthy talk, I would recommend that you factor in 5–10 minutes for questions at the end. However, for a short talk, consider the following strategy. Start by telling the audience during your introduction: 'As I have only 15 minutes to present this project to you and I know you will have questions, please can you...' plus one of the following options:

- ▶ '... write any questions down on the pads on the table, alongwith your name, and I will contact you later.'
- ▶ '... hang on to questions until right at the end and we will see how much time can be allowed.'
- ▶ '... email me your questions to the address on the handout and I will contact you.'
- ▶ '... write your questions on the whiteboard and I will look at them later.'
- ▶ '... ask the Chair to collate all questions and I will issue a FAQ sheet later on this week.'

If you set the 'rules' for questions at the beginning of your talk, you will not find yourself out of control later on. If anyone persists in wanting a question answered NOW, look to the Chair – they, after all, are managing the time aspect of the meeting.

Following your talk

After your talk is complete, it is highly likely that you will be required to leave the room, as the Chair will want to continue with the meeting and some items to be debated may be confidential. If you have equipment to pack up, the Chair may decide to call a short comfort break. If this happens do not interpret this as a time to help yourself to a cup of coffee or start a conversation with someone, this is time for you to pack up swiftly and go.

Thank the Chair (if possible) before you leave, and mention that you will be in touch in case any issues arise later in the meeting that refer to your presentation.

Now return to your office and reflect on the meeting. How did it go? How was your timing? Could you have improved any aspect?

From a practical angle, is there any information you need to send out to the group? If so, do it now, before you forget. Also send that email to the Chair, thanking them and asking if there were any issues raised after you had left.

As a final point of courtesy, if you want to make doubly sure that everyone has the information, you could also email the administrator with an electronic copy and ask them to send it out with the minutes. A further friendly touch would be to send an email to all the attendees, such as the one below:

To: Members of the Personnel Forum

Re: Presentation at the Personnel Forum on [date]

Dear Members of the Personnel Forum,

Thank you for allowing me to present my project at your meeting earlier today. As I am sure you will appreciate, the project was quite far-reaching and therefore in 15 minutes I was only able to touch on the aspects that I felt would impact on your business. However, if you would like to discuss these or any further details, please contact me on XXXX and I would be more than happy to meet you.

Regards,

Paul Lincoln.

Figure 6.3 Sample follow-up email from guest speaker.

KEEP IN MIND...

1 Being asked to speak in a meeting is a great way to get yourself noticed.

2 Preparation is essential to the task of pitching it right.

3 Never make assumptions – always check and question.

4 Be totally audience-focused – what do they need and want to know?

5 Plan a structure and lay it against your time allocation to see whether it flows and is possible.

6 Learn to talk to time – it is a useful skill that is hugely appreciated.

7 Any information you take with you should either complement or substantiate your presentation.

8 Don't get caught out – manage the way you deal with questions.

9 Thank the Chair and offer to speak again in the future.

10 Use follow-up methods to maintain contact and create a great impression.

7

....

Being heard in meetings

In this chapter you will:
- *identify ways in which you can make yourself more visible*
- *revisit vital communication skills*
- *consider creating impact with non-verbal triggers.*

The benefits of having a visible presence

Ever felt that you are not heard in meetings? That, although you are there and contributing, for some reason no one seems to notice you? If that is so, you are not alone. Many people tell me that they would like to increase their visibility in meetings and actually receive the credit for the ideas they bring to the table.

I am sure you will appreciate that having great ideas and insight is insufficient if you cannot convey those notions in a way that has them accepted as valid contributions. Like it or loathe it, we do look to others for confirmation that we have contributed something useful to the meeting, and if we don't get that confirmation, it is easy to feel, at best, invisible and, at worst, resentful and ignored. Neither of these is acceptable or conducive to effective working, and so they have to be recognized and dealt with accordingly.

There are very few people who do not mind another person snapping up their original idea and profiting from it, and yet this is what happens in meetings when you are not noticed or heard. Business is so competitive that people tend to guard their ideas carefully and choose the exact time and manner for revealing them. Even if you are fairly tolerant, it can be quite difficult to see someone else pick up your idea and present it as their own. I am sure you have seen this happen, even if you have not experienced it personally. Complain and you sound churlish; ignore it and you won't receive the credit – so what do you do? Far better to make sure that it does not happen in the first place.

Being heard in meetings has two strands:

1 the **presence** you have so that you can never be ignored
2 the **voice** you use, to actually be heard.

We will cover both aspects in this chapter, as a two-pronged approach that will cover most eventualities in this tricky arena.

However, first let's consider why it is important to have a visible presence. Being visible…

▶ increases the likelihood of your ideas being adopted
▶ identifies you as a person to be listened to
▶ validates the ideas you have
▶ gives credibility to your role at work
▶ demonstrates that you have a worthwhile role on this project or in the meeting
▶ ensures that you are seen as a 'solver of problems'
▶ allows you to have a greater say in how the organization makes its decisions and operates

…and most importantly, it quite simply *gets you noticed*!

It is at meetings that you have a chance to impress senior staff whom you may never work with at any other time. It is therefore an opportunity to shine and show others your incredible insight, creativity, problem-solving skills, and logical reasoning… None of this will come across if you are determined to blend into the wallpaper or only nod sagely at the comments of others.

If, as you are reading this, you think, 'My goodness, that's me! I don't make much of an impression in any of the meetings I attend,' I would urge you to consider not just your visibility during meetings but how you feel you come across in general. Let's look at four possibilities:

1 **Physically quiet people** – some people are just quiet and they prefer to blend into the background. Think about how you walk and present yourself. Are you always the last in the room? The one who pours the tea, closes the door, calls facilities? You could be giving hidden messages that you want to disappear or not be at the meeting without realizing it.

2 **Verbally quiet people** – these people have plenty of ideas, but do not like to push themselves forward. They are often more internally thoughtful and therefore consider the conversation deeply – but unfortunately, by the time they wish to speak, the conversation has moved on. There is no link between quietness and intelligence but quiet people are often overlooked or steamrollered in meetings. If you are naturally verbally quiet, it can be very difficult to compete with extroverts and so, rather than trying to talk more, make each statement you make important and impactful. If you need more time to think, ask the Chair whether it is possible to return to this item later.

3 **Feeling overwhelmed** – not everyone is comfortable in meetings; meetings can seem gladiatorial or full of conflict, which can feel very scary and overwhelming for some people. Add to that the fact that some meetings are held in impressive venues such as your director's office, and you are expected to think on your feet – and this can create a recipe for anxiety. If you feel overwhelmed by attending a meeting, you may need to consider undertaking some deep breathing exercises to help you relax, prior to entering the room.

4 **Not engaged** – do you really care about the subject matter of the meeting? If not, then you might just sit back and decide to opt out altogether. This is non-productive and can be a great distraction for others. If this feels familiar, question yourself as to whether there is any part of the meeting that you feel interested in. If not, then it might be better if you stayed away. Your lack of engagement may pull down the entire meeting and be interpreted as disruptive.

Some people believe that you cannot develop a presence; that, like charisma, you either have it or you haven't. However, I don't think that is necessarily fair or true. There are some things you can do to improve your presence and get more noticed.

Dress to impress

I have already mentioned the importance of dress but perhaps not delved into how it can help you and what you should be wearing.

The clothes you wear work in two ways:

1 As an **outward sign** to everyone as to who you are, how much you value your image and, in some cases, the level you are at in the organization.

2 As an **inward prop** for increasing your confidence and making you feel positive.

Whether you feel comfortable or not with this first statement, we make assumptions about people based on the clothes they wear. Some clothes or adornments even fuel those assumptions by sending very specific signals – for example religious adornments or badges. Be aware of the messages you are giving through your clothes and make sure they are the messages you want to convey. It is quite easy to change your image through clothes and therefore, if you feel that you do not emit sufficient presence in meetings, you can start by looking at your work wardrobe.

Be honest about your current work wardrobe – does it suggest someone who is highly visible in meetings or someone sitting back? Colours can help but they are not the only story. Wearing a flash of bright colour can get you noticed, and that can be in a pattern on a blouse or a stylish tie. Even in a company that wears basic, neutral colours, you can experiment with a scarf or coloured accessories. Most items (pens, notebooks, folders, phone cases, briefcases and even laptops) are available in a full range of colours, and you could have a signature colour that marks you out from the rest.

If you feel that you are not making a sufficient impact, look at what other people are wearing – but not those at your level; look to the level above. Also pick out someone who you feel has real presence and see whether you can pinpoint what it is in the way that they dress that either confirms or asserts that presence – and then copy it.

Good-quality, well-cut clothes will always be noticed, but do not think that this is all about money. There are some great 'replica' clothes these days that include the detail of more expensive items (such as overstitching); you just need to look for them. Another trick is to buy a good-fitting jacket from a regular clothes store and customize it – for example by changing the buttons. Suddenly it looks (and therefore you also look) unique and different.

The second point was that clothing can be an inward prop to increase our confidence. When you know that you look good, you walk a few inches taller, and project yourself differently. You feel assertive and authoritative, and this will mean that you take a more active part in the meeting, and feel comfortable putting forward your point of view.

Behaviour breeds behaviour

If you are to be heard in your meeting, you need firm, strong behaviour. Behaviour (or body language) is something that we take notice of *before* we even listen to the words being said. This means that you could be giving off the wrong signals before you have even opened your mouth.

Let's just think for a moment of how a strong, assertive person may present themselves in a meeting. They are more likely to...

▶ introduce themselves to others (not wait to be introduced)
▶ take control of the area as if it were theirs (even if they are a guest)
▶ appear organized and knowledgeable
▶ interrupt or disagree, but in a way that does not offend.

Is this you? If not, you really do need to rethink the way you behave in meetings. If you walk in behind others and try to blend into the background you will be perceived as a mouse and you will be treated accordingly. Similarly, if you act like the assistant you will be treated thus, even if you really have a crucial part to play in the meeting. Confidence is key here… but what if you feel anything less than fully confident?

Studies on behavioural psychology have shown that, when it comes to confidence, if you act confident, you will automatically start to feel far more confident. This is because your brain does not know the difference between your true feelings and the messages it receives. Therefore, because your body is sending it a message saying, 'I am confident', the brain will believe it.

You are now probably wondering how we give the brain these 'I am confident' signals – it is through our body language! Start by drawing yourself up to your full height. Stand tall and proud, and feel the power of being in control. Now smile and relax your shoulders a little. Take some deep breaths, in through the nose and out through the mouth, and imagine that with every out-breath, some of your concerns or insecurity flow out of you, leaving only the strong, good feelings behind. Use this technique every time you feel nervous or under stress.

Insight

Practise how to make an entrance with panache. Consider how you enter the room, your posture and the manner in which you carry documents and seat yourself. Have a well-practised introduction so that it is always ready, and learn how to give a firm and business-like handshake.

Vital communication skills

There are some basic communication skills that we need to observe in meetings:

INTRODUCTIONS

If you are invited to a meeting with people you do not know, it is customary to begin with a round-table set of introductions. Note: these are usually only your name and/or project title and role – for example, 'Pat Smith, Intereg Project Manager' or 'Chris Curby, representing ABC Pharmaceuticals'. Never go into longer detail – this is not a training course. If anyone needs to know more information about you, they will ask for a fuller outline.

MAKING COMMENTS

The Chair will introduce each item and then pass over to the 'item owner' to present or fill in the details. Allow the item owner to present their item without comment. They will usually open the item up for debate at the end. Each meeting will have its own unwritten code of conduct here, and you can learn a lot from watching how other people introduce their own comments.

OBJECTING OR DISAGREEING

This is very much dependent on the organization you work for or the prevalent behaviour in the meeting, and therefore, in the first instance, if you are at all unsure, watch other people. You would not want to shout out 'I OBJECT!' or 'NO!' and bang the table if that is not the way your company operates. In some organizations it is healthy to voice your objections fiercely and in others it is not (this is also true for different cultures). When you think a more measured approach is needed, consider using other phrases such as:

▶ 'I would like to challenge that – in my experience the opposite happened…'
▶ 'I am not sure that I agree with you on this point…'

- ► 'I have some experience in this and so I need more convincing arguments to win me over at this stage...'
- ► 'I understand your premise but I am afraid that I cannot be a party to that...'

These are all strong statements but delivered in a softer way, and, if you needed to step back and change your mind, it would be easy to return with your dignity intact, rather than if you had caused a scene.

SPEAKING UP

When you have a comment to make, ensure everyone hears it clearly. Not everyone has a loud voice but if you are too quiet your comment may be lost in the mêlée of other comments. If you are nervous, write down your comment before saying it, so that, if you dry up, you can look down at your paper. When you speak out, say your point clearly and concisely, and then await the response. It can be difficult to think on your feet but the more you practise the easier it will get, and you can always ask the Chair to intervene if things get out of hand.

WAITING FOR A LULL

If you are waiting for a lull in the meeting to make your point, it probably won't happen and you will never manage to intervene. Commenting can be quite competitive and therefore, if you hang back, the opportunity may never present itself. If you truly find that you cannot make your comment because of everyone talking at once, appeal to the Chair, or say in a loud voice, 'I would like to make a comment, please,' and you may find that everyone magically quietens down.

OTHERS CUTTING IN OVER YOU

This leads us on to other people who might interrupt you or cut across your comments. If you start to speak but someone immediately cuts in, don't start a fight. Remain as restrained and calm as possible, and then say in a moderate tone, 'Please, I was speaking.' This then exposes the other person as someone out of control of their impulses and overly impetuous. If it happens again (and it may be by the same person), appeal to the Chair by saying, 'I would like to finish my comment but I am experiencing some problems – should I continue?' This then puts the problem firmly in the hands of the Chair and they will either have to warn the other person who cut in or defer the item to another forum.

It happens to all of us at some point. We leave the room and then think of the very thing we wanted to say. You cannot call everyone back to the meeting again. If it is a huge issue (such as the budget figures being incorrect), seek the Chair out immediately and discuss it. If it is not that important but you wanted to make your point, issue a letter or email to the group, expressing the point you want to make about that one item, and ask for your comments to be added to the minutes if necessary.

Actions speak louder than words

Meetings can be very intense places where tempers are frayed and problems can be magnified. In such an atmosphere everything you do will be noticed and assumptions drawn. This section of the book is about being noticed but you don't want to be noticed for the *wrong* things, so be very careful of 'facial comments' such as rolling your eyes to the person next to you or shaking your head.

Where you sit can also speak volumes. If you want your presence noted, sit in the eyeline of the Chair, or that of the speaker of a particular item you have seen on the agenda and wish to specifically comment on. If you are someone who is a little shy, don't fuel this by hiding in the corners or behind someone else.

Tip

A note here about mobile phones. There is a disturbing habit emerging of people answering texts during meetings. This is rude and disrespectful to the person speaking on each item, and you are not really listening if you are texting. If you need to reply or accept an urgent text during a meeting, clear it with the Chair first and then announce that this might happen, so that everyone is aware.

Attending on your manager's behalf

From time to time you may be asked to attend a meeting on your manager's behalf. This is great kudos for you but may not be good news for the other people in the meeting, as the main decision maker is missing and you will have to go back and check everything with the original manager. However, to make the most of this situation there are a few points you can consider to smooth the waters. In the first instance, prepare!

Read the agenda and note any items that appear to be relevant to your department, and any that you really don't understand.

Find time to speak with your manager to discuss the agenda. Where there are items on which you may need to speak, ask your manager what stance they would like you to take and how much interaction they would like you to have (they may only want you to attend and take notes). Where there are items you do not understand, ask your manager for a quick update so that you at least understand the topic or its implications.

At the meeting, introduce yourself as a representative – for example: 'My name is Bill Smithers and I am standing in for Karen Cooper this morning.' If you are only going to take notes and not fully represent the views of Karen Cooper, you should say: 'My name is Bill Smithers and I am taking notes this morning for Karen Cooper who is unfortunately unable to attend.' This makes sure that everyone is aware of the situation.

If there are any items that you do not understand (and you have not been briefed on), simply make as many notes as possible so that you can give feedback to your manager and they can explain the issues later. This way you will be better prepared next time. Similarly, if there are items of interest mentioned that you may feel your manager might be very interested in, then also note these down for discussion later.

Following the meeting, have a full and frank feedback session with your manager (don't just rely on them receiving the minutes), discuss your comments and clarify any other issues from the meeting. Hopefully you will have learned some more details regarding your business and in that sense the meeting can be highly developmental for you.

KEEP IN MIND...

1 Try to create a visible presence – you want people to remember you.

2 Many people are offered promotions based on how senior staff members have seen them perform in meetings.

3 Dress appropriately and comfortably.

4 Dressing well does not need money but it does need thought.

5 Do not always wait to be introduced – step forwards.

6 If you wish to object to a point, do so politely.

7 Learn to deal with others cutting in or commenting while you are speaking.

8 Consider some of your body language during the meeting – is it effective/appropriate?

9 Welcome attending a meeting on your manager's behalf – it can be very developmental.

10 Always factor in pre- and post-meetings with your manager to clarify the details.

8

Follow-up

In this chapter you will:
- *find a more realistic way of managing the follow-up to meetings*
- *learn how to brief your manager in the most appropriate manner*
- *consider meetings as part of your personal development.*

Critical first steps

After a busy meeting you could be excused for going back to your desk and throwing all your notes in the ever-increasing pile that accumulates on your desk and forgetting about them. After all, you have another meeting this afternoon and you need to prepare for that. Sure you will get around to revisiting your notes, but the next meeting is weeks away yet – plenty of time. If this sounds spookily familiar, this chapter will help to sort you out!

If you are the super-person who organizes yourself after every meeting, then you have every right to feel pleased with yourself and to miss out this chapter altogether. However, in my experience, the behaviour outlined above is more common than you may think – though that does not make it any more acceptable. Like much in our life, we can improve, and the fact that the improvement could have other beneficial effects on our working lives must mean it's worth making the change.

In this chapter I will outline a follow-up that is simple and quicker to undertake than having a chat, and will provide you with more benefits. Sound interesting? Then here we go.

If you are the person mentioned above, happy to be back at your desk and yet very short of time, it is likely that, following the meeting, you will engage in one of two behaviours, following on from putting your papers in your 'pending pile'. You will *either*:

▶ go and make yourself a coffee, *or*
▶ have a quick chat with a friend.

The reason we do this is not just about wanting a drink or a conversation; it is largely psychological. We need breaks in routine to separate our life and thoughts, which then enables us to move onto the next piece of work with a clear head.

However, these breaks take time and that is something we might use more productively at this point in the day. I am certainly not saying don't have a drink or a conversation; I am just questioning whether this is the most appropriate time to do these things... and, let's be honest, the drink in the kitchen ends up being a chat, and the chat often ends up in you deciding to make a drink, and so the likelihood is that you end up doing both!

Let's consider a slightly different regime. You return from the meeting, go to your desk and sit down. Now, instead of tossing your notes onto the pile, you grab a highlighter and your diary (or PDA/scheduler). Now go back through your notes highlighting the sections where you need to perform an action or have an interest – even if you are not mentioned by name. Now, using your diary or PDA/scheduler block out time to consider, plan and undertake the actions mentioned, so that you can assess what can be achieved before the date for the next meeting. If at this point you think 'This is just impossible,' speak with the Chair immediately so that you are able to book an extension of time to appear in the minutes.

If you are in the fortunate position of having a PA or administrative assistant, brief them on any outcomes of the meeting that will affect your work or impinge on your time. You may also need their help in freeing up some time in your diary or taking charge of your phone for a period of time.

Now file your notes away in a place where you know you will be able to locate them easily. Again time is lost trying to locate notes that you know were in that pile somewhere. You might say, 'Well, what is a few minutes here and there,' but those few minutes add up and the next thing you know, you cannot find your papers and you are late for the meeting again – giving a very poor impression to everyone else.

The whole operation (outlined above) should have taken you no more than five minutes, no longer than making that cup of coffee. However, instead of creating a muddle, you have actually put a plan in action, and when that diary date to review the meeting comes up in a few days' time, you will know that it is time to tackle the actions allocated to you. It is a small change in behaviour that could save you many repercussions. I think you now deserve that drink and a chat, don't you?

Insight

It is very easy for us to fool ourselves that we are organized and coping well with our work until it's too late. Staying on top and in control of work is a skill that is vital at any senior level. You need to find a method that is right for you – and not all great ideas involve a lot of hassle. Some quick, simple ideas work very well and anything that will enable you to be more organized has to be worth trying.

Taking the message back

I mentioned earlier that you may be standing in for a manager or even the whole team. It is not unusual for a team manager to send one of the team to a meeting that they are unable to attend themselves, or as a developmental opportunity for staff. If this is the situation, then you will have to feed back the outcome of the meeting to the manager or whole team.

There are two main ways for doing this: in a follow-up meeting or by briefing note. We will look at each one in turn:

▶ **The follow-up meeting** – this will either be with the person who should have attended, or with the team. The benefit of discussing the outcome with the team is that you can tell everyone at once and the team can start the actions or integrating the information immediately. The downside of holding a follow-up meeting is that you need everyone to be present; otherwise you might have to repeat the information. Another problem that might present itself is that, part way through your commentary, you may be asked more questions and you will drift off the point. It is also quite time-consuming as there is likely to be debate, and this may waste time because the decision may have already been made in the meeting.

▶ **Feedback by briefing note** – this has some advantages in that it is consistent (the same message for everyone), can be left for staff even if they are not at their workstations, can be concise, and forms a written record (should something go awry later on). The downside of a briefing note is that it can be quite impersonal, holds a small amount of information, and takes arguably more effort to type it. Moreover, you cannot ask it questions and, if sent by email, you cannot be sure that everyone has read it.

You can type a briefing note in any format you choose. However, if the agenda has been sent to you in a computerized format, you can use that as a format for your briefing note, as shown in Figure 8.1.

Making actions happen

If you are attending a meeting, it is to be supposed that you are part of the business of the meeting. In other words, it is likely you are there for a reason, not just to while the time away. As I mentioned at the beginning of this book, meetings are a way of moving business forward, making decisions and allocating resources to projects. It is therefore highly likely that, as you are attending, you will be expected to contribute and put your name to the relevant actions emerging from the meeting.

Actions are simply that – a documented call for you to do something. That 'something' could be anything from a short:

> **Action: Samantha D to inform all staff of new policy**

to a rather more extensive action such as:

> **Action: Samantha D to write a report on the falling standards in product care**

As you can imagine, the first example might take only minutes and the second, weeks of hard work. The other point to be aware of is that you may be actioned in the minutes of meetings you have not attended. You are probably thinking – how would I know? Well, you only know when someone tells you or you suddenly receive a set of minutes. Therefore if some minutes appear in your in-box or on your desk and you do not recognize them – do not delete them or throw them away without flicking through them first. You may have been actioned in your absence!

Prodash Project Meeting

Meeting to be held: [date], at the PPR Offices, Wokingham

The Winslet Room, 15.00–17.00

Chaired by Andrea Cahill

AGENDA

Attendees: Linda Salmon, Rosalind Mitchell, Kirsty Mullings, Jim Broyle, Pete Marcus, Lois Jennings (minute taker)

Item number	Item	Time
1.	Introductions	15.00
2.	Overview of the work achieved so far – *Phase one completed, Phase two commencing soon, project on time and within budget*	15.05
3.	Implementation of the new plan – *New plan to be implemented 12 July 20XX, our part of the plan to commence 14 Aug 20XX*	15.20
4.	Signatories and first quarter payment details – *Does not concern our project*	16.00
5.	Future requests for funding – *Funding has been approved*	16.20
6.	Project summary document – *Attached to minutes*	16.35
7.	Action points collated – *we achieved all our actions*	16.45
8.	Date of next meeting agreed – *6 May 20XX*	16.55
9.	END	17.00

Figure 8.1 An agenda used as a format for a briefing note.

If this happens, there are two issues here:

1 What you have to do
2 How long it will take you.

First, check what it is that you actually need to do. Is it within the remit of your job, do you have the right qualifications or experience to do it, and are you the best person to carry out the action? It might mean you having a meeting with your manager to see how this action fits into your other areas of work and how you might achieve it.

The second point is the timescale. Usually people want actions completed as soon as possible, but how does that fit in with your other work? You can't 'make time' but time can be allocated to this action if you are able to redistribute your other work to fit it into your schedule. Again, you may need your manager's help and guidance on this.

Now the scheduling. If it is the second example given earlier (the report), estimate how much time you have available between now and the following meeting. (If writing the report requires you to contact other individuals, do not underestimate how long it takes to do this and for everyone to come back to you. Most people are very busy and encompassing other people's timetables can be quite difficult.)

When you have an estimation of the time involved, speak with your manager as to whether this is acceptable. Your manager may wish to negotiate with the Chair, or they may prefer you to negotiate with the Chair yourself. The most important issue is to gain agreement on a time frame for this project. The minutes can be amended to show this at the next meeting and the essential point is that the report gets underway.

Actions will only happen when they are diaried in and allocated the sufficient amount of time to make them happen.

Contact and follow-through

When you have a plan of how you will achieve your action, you need to make sure that it is communicated not just to the Chair but also to the person or group who raised the agenda item. It may be that you actually don't know that person or group and therefore you need to look them out and meet with them to discuss the outline. If your action item was to write a report on the falling standards in product care, I am sure you would want to know the background to this and also what the 'owner' of the action would like covered. This is often called the **specification** for the report. It is important to get this agreed; otherwise you may write your report in one way when another approach, altogether different, was needed.

From then on it is useful to keep everyone up to date with the progress of your report so that you are able to extend timescales if necessary. It would be a personal disaster if you did not deliver your action on time, as it would make you appear unprofessional. However, if you feel you need more time, and you flag it up early enough, something can usually be worked out.

Tip
If you are diaried an action that you have not agreed to or you were not at the meeting when this decision was made, do not immediately accept that you have to achieve it immediately. Speak with your manager, as there are grounds for negotiation here, and possibly even refusal.

Meetings and personal development

We think of meetings as a way of doing business but possibly not as a way of developing skills. However, by taking part in meetings you can develop:

- ▶ tact and patience
- ▶ the ability to analyse
- ▶ questioning and listening skills
- ▶ clear communication
- ▶ the ability to debate
- ▶ reasoning
- ▶ note taking
- ▶ time management / personal organization
- ▶ conflict skills
- ▶ professional conduct / self-management
- ▶ strategy
- ▶ skills centred on dealing with difficult people…

…all skills that are required in management, leadership, or for senior posts.

If you see your future as existing higher up in the organization, attend as many meetings as possible to enable you not only to gain those skills yourself but also to see them in action.

If you ever find yourself in a meeting in which you have either completed your section of the agenda, come as a guest, or discovered that the meeting is not one you should be at, rather than leave, carry out a little people watching and see if you can identify techniques that are used by the Chair and other members to move business along. (If you have the opportunity, another option is to ask if you could observe or shadow a senior manager in a meeting. You may find it very interesting – being an outsider at a meeting allows you to watch all the players as they operate, and (hopefully) enable you to identify good and poor practice.)

You may also be in the position of working towards a professional qualification. If so, reflecting on meetings and meeting styles and behaviours can form part of a continuing professional development (CPD) log or similar evidence of learning.

Attending meetings as part of your career strategy

Where do you want to be in ten years' time? Sitting around the table or at the head of it? If you have a career strategy that includes moving forwards (and upwards), then you need to identify those meetings that you need to attend. If you are not working on a key project, then you need to be seen to be someone who is useful to have at meetings, so that you are invited to the key ones and have a presence.

You need to make sure that you *always* have something to say at each meeting, not always easy when you are put on the spot and in a meeting where you don't really know the background. Try to do as much research as possible in advance of the meeting and aim to get a grasp of not only the issues on the agenda but also any background information that would support an argument either way. For example, for a new product launch you would need to know not only about the product but also how the business is doing financially. The financial security of the business selling the proposed product needs to be investigated with respect to whether it can afford to support a new product while it becomes established in the market.

Also helpful is to have a few stock replies just in case you are caught on the spot, such as 'This is very complex and I would not feel happy giving you a complete answer right now. I think the best thing to do would be for me to research the implications and come back to you' or 'Although I would like to give you an answer now, I need to do a little more research first.' That would, at least, save you face and buy you time! What you cannot be seen to do is to verbally stumble and have to admit that you do not understand the issue concerned.

If you really want to stand out from those around you, you can even offer to chair the meeting! If that appeals, there is a handy section in this book (Part four) telling you just how to do that. Chairing meetings is a great skill that, once mastered, can be used in all manner of situations and can definitely add to a CV or job profile. However, be warned. Read the section through carefully – there are good Chairs and poor ones. Make sure you are one of the former; otherwise you could find that you make the opposite impression to the one you intended!

KEEP IN MIND...

1 The meeting may end when you leave the room, but your responsibilities don't.

2 Put in place a system for organizing your workload so that you are able to manage your actions and file the paperwork away so that it is readily accessible.

3 Schedule or block out time in your diary to undertake the actions allocated to you.

4 If you do not have sufficient time to undertake an action, do not just leave things until the following meeting or muddle along, achieving only half of what you should – contact the Chair immediately.

5 Consider how you are going to feed back the outcome of the meeting. Which is the most appropriate method?

6 Just because you did not attend a meeting does not mean you cannot be actioned to do some work.

7 Maintain a close relationship with the person owning the action. They can help you greatly and may even extend the completion date if things become difficult.

8 Offer to attend meetings on behalf of your manager, whenever you can.

9 Meetings are a great way to develop your skills for senior management.

10 Think of meetings as a way of extending your career. Make sure you contribute and get yourself known.

Part three
Taking the minutes

9

....

Different types of minutes

In this chapter you will learn how to:
- *recognize the different types of minutes*
- *involve the relevant people in your discussions*
- *decide on the most appropriate format for your minutes in each case.*

Agreeing appropriate minutes

If you have been taking minutes for some time, or have been working in an environment where there is a proliferation of meetings, you will know that there are many different types (or formats) of minutes.

The choice of which way to record your minutes generally comes up when:

▶ there is a new meeting set-up to minute
▶ you recognize that the format currently used is not fit for purpose.

New meetings need to use a form of minute recording that is in line with the meeting itself. Formal meetings will need far more detail and conformity than social meetings. There is usually less tension around selecting the format here. However, it may be slightly more contentious to attempt to change the type of minutes used by an already established group as you run the risk of not only giving offence but also running into the 'but that's the way we have always done it' crowd – people who don't like change. This can be tricky but it is not insurmountable, and you might find that your professionalism requires you to put forward other templates or ideas. And, of course, once embedded, your 'new' ideas soon become 'the way things are done around here'.

In most cases, if you have taken over the minute taking from someone else, you will probably find copies of their minutes on the office computer and you will be able to use the same template. However, it is good to be alert to the varying types of minutes so that you can make suggestions.

One final point: some organizations prefer their minutes to be recorded in a specific way and/or on letterhead/company paper. If this is the case, you may have little leeway for discussion.

Your minutes must be appropriate for the meeting and also must be agreed with the Chair and, in some instances, the 'stakeholders'. The term stakeholders simply means anyone who has a vested interest or input into the meeting. Where a meeting is being led firmly from the front – perhaps by a manager who is acting as Chair – it will be their sole decision. However, if the meetings are run co-operatively, perhaps by a project team, everyone might want a say in how the minutes should be presented. Another instance where negotiation would be involved is in a joint meeting. If the meeting were to detail a merger or where organizations are working in partnership, the format of the minutes may need to be agreed by both parties.

Agreeing minutes in this way can save you a lot of time later on, so if you are in charge of minute taking, always make sure that you know exactly which type of minutes you will need to take for this specific meeting. For example, if you do not need verbatim minutes, you will not need to write everything down – only some notes and the actions. However, if you had written only summary notes and found out later that verbatim minutes were expected – you might be in a spot of bother.

Tip

A note on style. Many organizations are now investing in an holistic approach to their marketing and brand. This includes how minutes are presented. Before redrafting a new layout, take time to find out whether your organization has a style format that you need to adhere to.

Minutes for informal meetings

Informal meetings can cover any subject. They could be for a regular team meeting or for a group of people brought together to discuss some issue that probably won't be publicized, such as where the Christmas dinner might be held this year!

They are informal for several reasons:

► People may know each other well (and therefore there need not be introductions).
► The way everyone acts is informal, and there may not even be a 'formal' Chair.
► The subject matter is informal.
► The meeting warrants notes to record decisions but not legal details or a script of exactly what is said by each person.

Minutes of informal meetings need to capture the *essence* of the meeting together with any actions and dates, but need not be in a rigid style. Look at Figure 9.1. This is an informal team meeting with a few people attending who all know each other.

Structured minutes

As opposed to an informal style, there are occasions when minutes need to have a formal structure. These are possibly what we think of when we picture in our minds a set of traditional minutes.

Structured minutes generally follow the agenda and therefore each item is numbered so that the two documents link to each other. They also often (although not always) have an action column on the right-hand side to enter the action that is required, the person responsible and the date by which it should be taken.

The traditional structure lends them a gravitas that is not present in informal minutes, and immediately makes them appear important.

Note that in the (very short) example in Figure 9.2, the attendees (and also those who did not attend) are listed, whether they know each other or not. This is so that everyone is aware of who was present when each decision was made or action was recorded.

Minutes of Promotions Team Meeting – [date]
Landsdown Room, The Tower, London

Item 1 – The Public Suggestion Scheme

There was support for the newly proposed Public Suggestion Scheme which will commence in August. It is hoped that the scheme will generate more ideas for future promotions as well as providing valuable feedback.

To encourage suggestions, it was decided to offer a daily draw for a set of four free tickets which could be used in any attraction. This should not incur any direct cost to the attraction.

It was discussed that some of the winners could be photographed and used for future marketing. Costs and practicalities need to be estimated.

Action: Peter Charles to take this forward and report back at the next meeting

Item 2 – Changes to the way in which coach parties are booked

There will be a new way for coach parties to be managed, and from July all coach parties need to be met by a member of the Hospitality Team and directed through to the South Door.

This will ensure that they are kept away from the main entrance and that the party stays together. This is particularly important for school coach parties.

This will run as a pilot during June and will be managed by Samantha Brown in the expectation that it will be fully implemented for July, when the attraction moves into its busiest season.

Action: Samantha Brown to pilot this in June with a view to it becoming regular practice in July

Next meeting will be held on [date] in [venue].

Figure 9.1 Example of informal minutes.

Minutes of Mid-Angolian Children's Framework Meeting

Held on 14 November 20XX at Sunrise Building, 10 a.m.

Present:	Paula Fischer (chair)	**Apologies:**	Kathie Sidcup
	John Dhal		
	Pat Lincoln		
	Petra Disney		
	Lucy Hughes		
	Andrew MacFarlane		
Speakers:	Polly Brown	CRFT	

1 CRFT
Polly Brown, Senior Project Worker, working for CRFT, attended the meeting to catch up with the team. Her presentation is attached.

No Action

2 Minutes from previous meeting
Handout – John and Lucy had worked together on the recommendations of the 'Childhood in Mid-Angolia' document that should be available to all staff. They distributed it for consideration.
IT – new dates are now coming out for IT/IS training.
Team update – There has still been no confirmation from the Minister of Justice to come and speak to us concerning his role.

No Actions outstanding

3 Leave/work-shadowing
Can everyone please put forward their requests for leave for the coming six months. Many thanks. Jill had an interesting account of her experience work-shadowing Phil Mahew last month. Phil has agreed to another member of staff also work-shadowing him – if you are interested, please put your name forward.

Action – everyone by end of May
Action – Phil to collect and organize by mid-May

NEXT TEAM MEETING WILL BE ON 28 DECEMBER 20XX – GREEN HILL OFFICES AT 10 A.M.

Figure 9.2 Example of structured minutes.

Minutes for telephone meetings and video conferencing

We live in a technological age and increasingly technology is being used to take the place of formal face-to-face interaction. Holding a meeting is an expensive activity, especially when attendees have to travel. It is therefore very possible that your organization is experimenting with telephone meetings, conference calls and video conferencing. These can be very different to administer and minute.

Let's start by considering telephone meetings and conference calls. The main problem here is that of differentiation. How do you know who is speaking and how many people are on the line?

If you have the opportunity, try to minute a small meeting first, just so that you get the gist of how the equipment works and its capabilities. On most systems, each meeting attendee dials into a central number at a given time. The unique number connects them to a joint line and an automatic voice tells you that 'Phil Jones has joined the meeting'. By tracking this you will know when everyone is present and on the line. Unless you are using a video camera, you cannot see anyone and therefore you are dependent on each person giving their name EACH TIME they speak. Thus a typical conversation might go:

> 'Phil Jones speaking – I think that is a great idea. What do you think, Andy?'
> 'Andy McCall – I agree with you, Phil, but what about the outright decision; who will take responsibility for that?'
> 'Jane Mason – can I come in here? I think a decision of this type needs to go to the board.'

This is very helpful for you because not only do you know who is speaking each time but the system will often record the phone call for you. If you can then play it back through speech-recognition software, you may only have to check over the minutes to make sure they are accurate. However, there are occasions when the speakers are so fired up that they forget to say their names. If this happens, and you are unable to work out on the recording who spoke, you may conclude that it would have been easier to have been in the room as you could then have at least used visual clues.

For this reason telephone meetings must be very structured in their format (even if the minutes are not). Although I have heard of telephone meetings for 30 people, it is helpful to start with a small meeting and see how this works out for you.

Video conferencing can set other challenges. Yes, you can see everyone's face and expressions but, because of this, contributors stop saying their name, and the camera may be on the wrong person, especially if someone cuts across and makes a comment when someone else is speaking. It is fair to say that, although video conferencing is not new, it is not widely in use at the present time and therefore we still make mistakes when using it, such as turning away from the camera or turning to speak to someone else in the office while in the meeting.

Both of these are quite distinct in the way they affect minute taking and so it can often help to have a practice in advance of a real-life event. However, telephone meetings and video conferencing are the way forward and therefore it helps to be aware of the issues and how to work with their limitations.

Verbatim minutes

Verbatim minutes are literally that – as minute taker you need to transcribe everything that is said. This can put a lot of pressure on the minute taker (we will discuss how to speed up your writing in Chapter 10), but this pressure is not just about having to transcribe all speech at speed; it also includes maintaining your attention and having a good understanding of what is happening during the meeting. The contents of some meetings are just so interesting (especially if there is a human element) that it is easy for the minute taker to become wrapped up in what is being said, rather than in capturing the content. It can be like witnessing a TV soap in front of your eyes, and some meetings can become very emotional. Therefore being able to maintain a distance and concentrate only on the words said becomes very important.

Normally when we are taking minutes we may only transcribe a shortened form of the conversation. For example, for a 15-minute full and lively discussion involving six people regarding whether to change stationery supplier, you might minute:

There was considerable discussion regarding who should provide
stationery in the future and whether it was worth changing
supplier. The outcome was to stay with the current supplier but
to attempt negotiating a 10-per-cent discount for bulk orders.
Action KC.

In other words, you would not minute everything that was said as
part of the discussion, only a broad description with any action.
However, had verbatim minutes been requested for this meeting, you
would have tried to capture everybody's comments.

Verbatim minutes are usually taken during legal meetings and
negotiations and in detailed discussions where conflict is possible.
The accuracy of the minutes is critical because, after the meeting,
they are the only tangible record of what actually was said or
happened (unless there was a recording), and the case, deal or
negotiation may collapse if the minutes are not correct.

Case conferences and public meetings

Case conferences are meetings where everyone is there to discuss a
case in an effort to find a way forward. Unlike an informal meeting
(or some team meetings), everyone there has something vital to
say regarding the case, and they all have their own perspective and
specialism. For example, at a case conference to discuss the care of a
child there may be the child's parents, extended family, doctors, social
workers, authority officials and so forth – in fact, anyone who has
(or had) an input in the child's welfare and life both in the past and
as proposed for the future.

Case conferences need verbatim minutes to be taken. However,
they differ in that, when the minutes are typed up, they need to
fit a template so that the resulting report reads like a narrative.
To explain this, let me take you back a step. People don't talk in a
logical sequence. At a meeting like this the debate would probably
start with a report on the current situation before moving on to a
discussion on the options for the future while every so often delving
into the past situation. The meeting may regularly span these three
spectrums – past, present and future – but not in a logical sequence.
As a verbatim minute taker you need to note everything down, but
when you come to write up the case conference, you will find that,

using the prescribed format, there is a section that deals only with the past (i.e. the background to the case). To complete this section, you may need to go through all your notes several times extracting issues and information from the child's past that run throughout your notes. The other sections will need the same level of analysis, concentration and detail. This means that you will have to read through your notes several times to ensure the resulting report covers everything, which is why it can take a day or more to produce the final minutes or report for a meeting of this type. The minutes/report, when complete, become a legal document and now read like a life story and flow in a logical sequence. Do not let this alarm you; it is the job of the Chair to ensure that the resulting minutes are a record that is fit for purpose.

Public meetings are similar. They may be held in the community or some central location and adverts may have been posted. Council meetings are public meetings, as would be a meeting called to discuss whether, for example, the new Tressons supermarket should be built in Anytown. Anyone has a right to attend, and some of the meetings can become raucous or highly charged. If you are asked to take the minutes of a meeting like this, I would advise you to look through previous minutes and work-shadow a colleague prior to the event to see how certain points are noted. For example, are swear words included? Do you note interruptions? What do you minute if a speaker is late or does not turn up? If you work for a council or public body, there are rules regarding these issues.

Insight

Where there are likely to be a large number of people that you do not know, try to manage the situation. Consider name badges or nameplates – with the latter, make sure the writing is large enough for you to read from across the room. If someone speaks and you do not know their name, do not feel embarrassed to ask. If you are to record the minutes effectively, you need to know exactly who said what. (In public meetings it is common for each speaker to say their name first before making their point.)

If there are going to be formal introductions, draw up a seating plan and write the names in the place of where everyone is sitting.

KEEP IN MIND...

1 First review the style of minutes that are currently in operation – are they fit for purpose?

2 Only change format if you feel strongly that the wrong format is being used. You could cause offence, and you would not want to risk this unless it was important.

3 Speak to the Chair about how they would like the minutes to be presented.

4 If you are new to your organization, find out now if there is a set way of presenting minutes.

5 Informal minutes need only statements or notes, with action points.

6 If you need to take minutes for a telephone or video conference, try to minute a small meeting first by way of practice.

7 Never rely solely on a tape recording; you may not know who is speaking.

8 Each minuted entry should be linked to the relevant agenda item.

9 Minutes are not always written up in the order in which they are transcribed.

10 Do not feel that you cannot interrupt and ask someone their name.

10

Your role in the process

In this chapter you will:
- *identify the key roles that the minute taker needs to undertake*
- *learn how to organize and prepare for a meeting*
- *consider short cuts to your minute taking.*

Booking rooms and facilities

Now that you are aware of the different types of minutes and the reasons for applying each, we need to explore the minute taker's role in the whole process. How many times have I heard someone say 'I'm only here to do the minutes' or 'I am just the minute taker' as if this were a minor part in the process! When, in fact, the minute taker is probably the most important person in the room as they provide the lasting record. From a professional point of view, being able to take minutes is a hugely valuable skill that you can take with you into almost any sphere. People who can take minutes effectively are usually welcomed into any organization.

The role of the minute taker (and what that entails) varies in each organization. In some organizations, if you are informed that you will be the minute taker for that particular set of meetings, it will be anticipated that you will also set up the meetings and deal with the accompanying administrative tasks. In another organization it may be assumed that the meetings are organized by the Chair and that your role is purely to turn up and take the minutes. If you are not sure how your organization operates, find out now, so that there is no confusion later on.

However, as this job often falls to the staff member who is taking the minutes, we will also cover the administrative tasks here (see Part one for more detail).

In the first instance you will need to check whether the meeting, if it is regular, will use the 'usual' room. If that is the case, then there is often a booking procedure in place to ensure that you secure the room for that particular time, date and duration. Should there be a change in room, then you will be expected to find somewhere else. The Chair may decide to change rooms for a host of reasons including:

▶ **fairness** – to ensure that negotiations do not benefit one party by virtue of their always being on 'home ground'
▶ **unsuitability** – perhaps the current room is too stuffy, or there is insufficient parking and so on
▶ **size** – the meeting attendees may have increased in number
▶ **cost** – using a hotel may not have been a problem at the beginning but, now that funds are a little low, the budget manager may have told the Chair to find somewhere less expensive
▶ **change in facilities** – perhaps a room is required that has a stage or presentation equipment for a guest to use

...in addition to others. If you need to change the room, you are then in a similar position to someone who is booking a meeting room for the first time.

Some of the issues you need to consider are:

▶ **the number of people due to attend** – most rooms are designed to hold a certain number of people and exceeding that number may cause health and safety issues, as well as being uncomfortable
▶ **whether your company has any spare rooms** – as this is usually the most cost-effective option
▶ **the degree of confidentiality** – some rooms have very thin walls and everything discussed can be overheard (the noise from outside, too, can be very distracting)
▶ **the length of the meeting** – there may be some rule concerning how long you may have the room for
▶ **the time of the meeting** – the meeting may be outside usual working hours and sometimes access can be a problem – for example, would your office be open at 7 a.m. to host a breakfast meeting?
▶ **setting** – some managers have a certain affinity for particular venues
▶ **equipment** – even in this technological age, not all venues offer the provision of even a flip chart and stand, let alone data

projectors and sophisticated sound systems. Additionally, not all rooms can accommodate technology (I have come across rooms that did not even have plug sockets!)

▶ **the provision of hospitality** – will the meeting require a waiter/waitress service? Lunch or a meal? Will water be available in the room?

▶ **the budget** – is cost an issue? If it is, then you may be tasked with trying to find low-cost options such as enquiring whether other local businesses, schools, community projects and so forth have rooms available.

▶ **the cancellation procedure** – be aware of the cancellation procedure for your room. You may find yourself locked into an agreement that means you have to pay for the room even if you cancel, where you have not given sufficient notice. Also, whether you have paid for the room or not, if you no longer need it, make sure you cancel it so that others can take advantage of it now being free.

Setting and distributing the agenda

Once you have the venue booked, you can add the details to the agenda. It may be your role to raise the agenda (or it may be the Chair's), so check this out. If it is down to you and this is a regular meeting, you can begin by locating the last set of minutes and flicking through them. You can instantly see which items need to be placed back on the agenda for a progress report or because the outcome could not be decided. Look for comments such as:

▶ 'To be moved to the following meeting'
▶ 'An update on this project to be given at the next meeting'
▶ 'Contact from company not able to attend today, move to next agenda'.

When you have a 'skeleton' agenda containing these items you can top and tail it with any known guest slots, a section entitled 'Minutes from previous meeting' and then a 'Date of next meeting' (at the end). This can then be sent to the Chair for them to add any of their own items or ones that they know about.

Creating a skeleton agenda like this is very helpful as the Chair will not always remember what was outstanding from the last meeting. If you do this, they will then have very little to add and not only does the job become a quick one, but it also triggers the beginning of a professional and trusting relationship with the Chair – something we will talk about in more detail a little further on.

> **Tip**
>
> The Chair may also want to contact certain people to ask whether they have any agenda items they wish to include. All this takes time and therefore you need to make sure you have built in sufficient time capacity to do all this. If another agenda item crops up (or is even cancelled) just before the meeting, it is quite acceptable to hand out up-to-date agendas at the meeting itself, but it is not good practice to do this every time as it implies that you (and the Chair) are not sufficiently organized.

Once the agenda has been finalized with all the details (including the venue you have booked), it can be sent out. Most agendas these days are emailed out to attendees, but if you are sending out a notice to the general public or to other companies, you may not know their email address and therefore you may have to use a postal system. If that is the case, do make sure you leave sufficient time for the letter to arrive, and for them to confirm their attendance before the meeting.

It is not always general practice to ask for confirmation of attendance but, if you do, not only will you know who you are expecting (in case you want to create name badges or an attendance list) but you will also know numbers for catering.

Distributing separate papers

Quite often there will be a number of 'papers' that will need to be distributed with the agenda. These papers may be the previous minutes (although, if urgent, these may need to go out ahead of the agenda) or other pre-read material that is necessary for the meeting. The key aspect here is to bring everyone's attention to them. It is very easy to miss an attachment and therefore make a note of it on the agenda and also in the accompanying email or letter. For example, you could write:

Please find attached the agenda for the Regeneration Meeting next week together with the paper 'Regeneration in the Twenty-first

Century' which has been issued to provide background information. The Chair has requested that you find time to read this document in advance of the meeting as many of the issues being discussed at the meeting emerge from this highly influential paper.

As some of the accompanying files may be quite large you may need to consider 'zipping' (compressing) them into smaller files before emailing them. You may have large-capacity computers at work but the recipient may *not,* have and the attachments may either not be received or take forever to download into the recipient's in-box. Many organizations impose size limits on in-boxes and, in extreme situations, large files can clog up computer software and lock the computer (or smartphone) of the recipient. Another option is to place any papers on the company website from where they can be downloaded by anyone; however, depending on the confidentiality status of the papers, you may also have to issue a password to prevent all members of the public being able to access them. Whichever method you choose, try to ensure that the process is as easy as possible; otherwise people will avoid doing it and this is not the best way to build communication links with others.

Some papers will not be in electronic format and so may need photocopying and distributing by post. If this is the case, you may want to clarify whether the agenda then goes out in the post, too (to keep the information together), or whether you send the agenda by email and tell everyone to look out for the papers in the main mail. It can be confusing when documents are being sent to you from different directions and therefore clarity and organization are absolutely essential.

A note about copyright

If documents are covered by copyright, you cannot simply copy and distribute them without the author's permission. For example, you must not photocopy pages of a book – suggesting them for pre-reading prior to the meeting – without the publisher's or author's permission.

Inviting guest speakers

If there are guest speakers at the meeting, it may fall to you to send out the formal request. Again some managers or Chairs will want to do this themselves, or they may ask you to co-ordinate this.

If you are asked, ensure you have all relevant information upfront, before issuing the invitation. You need to know:

- ► who they are and how to contact them (name, project, department, company)
- ► whether a specific person is requested or anyone from that department/project
- ► which specific meeting they are requested to attend (your Chair may run several)
- ► (briefly) the reason for being invited and any specific focus or angle they need to have
- ► which time slot has been allocated to them
- ► whether it is intended that they stay or whether they should leave following their slot.

When you have all this information, try to contact the guest(s) as soon as possible – everyone's diary soon fills up and, if you leave it until the last minute, there is a greater chance that they will not be able to attend. Send either a letter or email like the one below:

To: Mark Hutchins
Subject: 'Regeneration in Our Communities' meeting

Dear Mr Hutchins,
There is to be a quarterly meeting of the project 'Regeneration in Our Communities' and I have been asked by my manager, Sylvia Hinchcliffe (who will be chairing the meeting), to see whether you would be available to attend the first section of the meeting, **at 9 a.m. on 23 July 20XX,** to provide a short presentation on the use of compost bins.

Ideally, she would like a ten-minute presentation followed by five minutes of questions, very similar to the talk you did recently for the Joint Communities project. Therefore we are looking altogether for no more than 20 to 25 minutes of your time. Would that be possible? If so, please contact me directly, and we can then discuss the finer details.

Many thanks,
Carol Carter

In essence, you need to give the speaker enough detail to make the decision regarding whether to attend, but not so much that you flood them with information when they have not yet accepted.

Once you have their acceptance, you need to contact the guest speaker again to arrange the finer details including:

▶ maps and contact names/numbers
▶ what they should do when they reach the company building (Will there be a parking space? Will they be expected at reception? Should they report to anyone? How do they locate the room?)
▶ their needs regarding equipment (laptops, leads, projector)
▶ whether any handouts are required
▶ whether any information has to be distributed in advance of the meeting.

Unless they are familiar with your organization and the premises, it can be quite daunting to turn up at a building where you have to give a talk, only to find out that you are not sure where to go or what to do. Therefore try to think of every eventuality. They are your guests and the impression you give says a lot about your organization.

At the meeting

At the meeting it is likely that you will be expected not only to take the minutes but also undertake some general organizational work. For example, if you have booked the room and facilities, then you are responsible for ensuring it is all fine on the day. To be sure, arrive early and bring with you a copy of any booking forms or emails confirming the details – just in case. If you can gain access to the room before the meeting, ensure that it is set up in the way you have requested, and confirm that any refreshments are on their way. Ensure that reception (and/or security) have a list of expected attendees and that they know how you would like to collect them from reception or whether to send them to the room. (If you are expecting a guest, then leave a message with reception to let them know how to reach you when they arrive.)

If possible, organize immediately where you and the Chair will sit. Ideally, as minute taker, you should sit next to the Chair – either to their left or right. The reason for this is so that, even during mid-meeting, you can pass a message or whisper to the Chair if there is anything that you did not hear, cannot understand or are confused by. If you are sitting elsewhere in the room, it might be difficult to catch the eye of the Chair and the moment may be lost.

It is customary to bring a couple of copies of the agenda with you and also a copy of the minutes from the previous meeting. This is so that, if anyone has forgotten to bring their copies (and this includes the Chair), there will be at least one copy in the room. Also bring along any other notes or copies of slides perhaps requested by the guest(s).

Insight

If you know that a guest or anyone else will be joining the meeting late, keep a chair free for them. It is nerve-wracking enough for anyone to have to walk into a room of people already engaged in conversation without there being nowhere to sit. Reserve them a seat and automatically you appear organized and your guest will feel 'expected'.

Throughout the meeting you will need to monitor the time and so either sit where you can see a clock or wear a clear wristwatch. Your role is to support the Chair in addition to taking the minutes, and this may include minor courtesies such as offering refreshments and looking after any guests.

Writing at speed

One of the skills of minute taking is undoubtedly the ability to capture information quickly and accurately. If you have been trained in shorthand, you will have no problem, but unfortunately shorthand is not as popular as it used to be and there are fewer people taking up the opportunity to learn. This can be seen in the reduced number of managers requesting it. Although it is useful, it is no longer seen as vital, and other skills such as familiarity with computers and project management have taken its place as modern must-haves.

However, that does not take away from the fact that, as minute takers, we still need to record at speed. There are many books on speedwriting available for those who wish to learn, but there are also some easy ways you can teach yourself to write at a faster speed:

▶ Reduce everyone's names to their initials – for example 'KC' instead of Karen Carter. (Just a word of warning – make sure there are no duplicates; otherwise you will not remember whether the point was made by Karen Carter or Kira Connelly!)

▶ Take short cuts and create a squiggle, shape or line for a whole sentence or project name. You do not want to write something like that out in full every time it is mentioned. For example, 'KC ~ ' could stand for 'Karen Carter from the Bridgetown Water Co-operative said...' or 'ß' could stand for 'motion carried'.

▶ Use a symbol for words that you commonly use – for example, use 'ā' for 'accommodation'. If you work in the hotel industry, you would be using this word all the time and you would not want to keep writing it in full.

▶ Lose the 'ing' and shorten some words that just don't need to be that long, such as 'trg' for training, 'bng' for beginning, 'fshg' for fishing and 'gdng' for gardening.

▶ Borrow from mathematical and computer shorthand – use @ for 'at' and < for 'more than' (or 'greater/bigger than/increasing'). Think about others you could use.

▶ Remove the vowels embedded within words and also use phonetics – u wll stll undrstnd wht is wrttn.

▶ Use text language. It can be fast and you are probably used to reading it back effectively.

Tip

A word of warning here – type up your notes as soon as possible following the meeting, as what may have seemed a sensible shortened form in the meeting may be unintelligible a week later!

KEEP IN MIND...

1 Make sure you are clear as to the duties your role as minute taker includes.

2 Allow plenty of time for bookings – space always seems to be at a premium.

3 Stay on the right side of the Facilities Department and they will help you.

4 Never forget to cancel a room if you no longer need it.

5 Always ensure guests know how to enter the building and have some contact names and numbers – just in case.

6 Keep a seat free for guests so that they appear welcome and expected.

7 Sit to the right or left of the Chair.

8 You have a valuable role to play at the meeting, so make your presence known.

9 Make up your own abbreviations for long strings of words – such as the project or team name.

10 Any techniques to help you write faster are only effective if you are able to read the information back again.

11

....

Structuring minutes

In this chapter you will:
- *consider the way that minutes should flow*
- *recognize the need for maintaining a style and tense*
- *be clear regarding decisions, actions, layout and numbering.*

Meeting versus audience

You have taken your notes of the meeting and you are justly feeling proud of yourself – after all, job done! Oh no, my friend. I am afraid that now begins the task of beating several pages of scribbled notes into well-ordered and well-structured minutes.

Structuring your minutes is an essential part of creating a document that is both easy to read and act upon. Everyone is too busy to mine for information. If the minutes are too complicated or confused, they will be consigned to the pile of 'things to read later' and there they will stay. In creating an interesting and balanced set of minutes, you are encouraging the readership and increasing the likelihood of the actions occurring. After all, as a meeting attendee, a sloppy and confused set of minutes would be the perfect excuse for why I haven't undertaken the actions requested of me, if indeed I needed one.

Structuring is also important because it helps with the ease of reading and researching later on – for example, if you are trying to find out why a decision was made (perhaps a planning decision). If you were able to locate the accompanying agenda, it will point to the name and date of the meeting. The minutes for that meeting (which links directly to the agenda) will now contain that item, together with the outcome and any accompanying notes. In essence, you are producing a paper trail that interconnects, and this has to make retrieval of information much easier.

Let's start by considering speech. Earlier, I mentioned that the way in which people speak is not how speech is reported (for a start, we are not going to be typing up every line with speech marks). This means that imposing a structure may mean that we have to adjust our presentation to knit the two aspects together – the words said, and the manner in which we want to present the material.

In the meeting everyone is interacting and people often follow on from each other without restating the facts. In other words, comments are given in relation to other comments. For example:

Person A: 'I think we should talk to Paula about this…'
Person B: 'Yes, she is the right person.'
Person C: 'What about Ben? He is very knowledgeable.'
Person A: 'Yeah, Ben then. Ben it is!'

You can see that all this makes sense only if you were to read all the speech and even then only if you understand the context. The last comment means nothing on its own and relates only to the comments before it. This is why you should never take quotations out of context. In the meeting it would be easy to follow this conversation and understand what the people are talking about, but when you are writing minutes you are writing them for an audience, and therefore they need to be given a context and a sense of flow that may not have actually been present during the discussion.

When we speak, we not only use words but we also communicate by:

▶ **non-verbal means** – for example nods of the head
▶ **noises** (or **interjections**) such as 'um', 'er' or 'ah!'
▶ **nonsensical speech** – 'Do you?' or 'Never!'
▶ **unfinished sentences** – 'I thought I might… no, don't worry.'

We may start a sentence speaking to one person and then finish it speaking to another! This would not make sense if written down and that is why, if you pick up any novel, speech is written not in the way we use it in everyday life but in a more formal style so that we can follow who is saying what and keep track of the story.

Minutes (unless verbatim) are there to give an overview of the meeting with any important points included or, in some instances, highlighted. This is very much like a story in a book. That is because you are now writing for an audience, and it has to be understood by people who were not even present.

If I were to minute the conversation quoted earlier, I would write:

Item 12 – The new office design	
There was some discussion regarding who would be best placed to advise on the design of the new office. It was agreed that at this stage Ben was the most appropriate person to comment.	Action: A to contact Ben

---

Insight

I am sure you have heard someone in a meeting say 'I want that minuted' in reference to a comment or decision that was made. Important points must be minuted to stand out from other comments which you intend only to précis.

Style, tone and tense

The **style** of your minutes can vary considerably and it is dependent on:

► **personal choice** (yours or that of the Chair) – you or they may like brief notes or bulleted entries
► **whether they are content-led** – you should adopt the most appropriate style for the content – probably notes for an informal meeting and structure for a more formal one
► **whether they are organization-led** – you should use the most appropriate style for your organization – for example, in a parish council there is usually a strict structure to observe, complete with numbering system.

Based on this choice, think how your minutes are presented for each of the different meetings you attend. Are you using the most appropriate style?

Now let us consider **tone** and **tense**. Minutes should be professional. Many minutes become documents that are viewed by other organizations or the public, and therefore the tone you set, as a minute taker, will be judged by all. As a rule of thumb, minutes should be written in the third person and in the past tense. What this means is that the minute taker is writing like a narrator telling a story about something that happened yesterday. For example, if you were telling a story you would say: 'Little Red Riding Hood went into the woods to get to her grandmother's house...' In the same way, your minutes would read:

> Little Red Riding Hood addressed the Chair concerning how to get to her grandmother's house via the shortest route. The Chair put it to the vote and it was suggested that she tried the route via the woods.

Silly maybe, but let's have an example that is a little more realistic:

Try this
Read through the following conversation between three people:
Person 1: 'I think we need somewhere else to hold these meetings.'
Person 2: 'Yes, it is becoming more difficult to get access to this room as more businesses are moving into the building.'
Person 1: 'It was OK when it was just us and TJ Holdings. They hardly used the room at all and did not appear to have meetings; now two more companies have moved in, it is getting harder.'
Person 3: 'What do these companies do?'
Person 2: 'One is a firm of solicitors and the other a firm of accountants, and they both have meetings all the time.'
Person 3: 'It is a shame that we have to move out; after all, we were here first.'
Person 2: 'Yes but the agreement of the rent is that the meeting room is shared by all those in the building, and so they have as much right to use the room as we do.'
Person 1: 'Anyone got any suggestions?'
Person 3: 'Well, I know someone who uses the hotel over the road and they say it is not too expensive.'
Person 1: 'I have to be over there next week. How about I look into it?'

Now, without reading on, write out how you would report this conversation in your minutes.

You should have something like:

Item 1	
There was a conversation regarding future venues for meetings now that the room is often booked by other organizations. A suggestion was made to use a room in the hotel opposite and [name] agreed to look into it.	**Action: [Name] to check prices and availability of rooms in hotel opposite.**

Your response does not have to be exactly like mine but hopefully you can see from my example that all of the speech has been put into the context of someone listening to the conversation but nonetheless detached from it. It is also written in the past tense ('There *was*...' 'A suggestion *was* made...').

Another point here to note is that, in my example, I did not particularly point out who came up with the idea of the hotel. If someone had said, 'Could you note that I made that suggestion,' I would have included a name, but, unless this is stated, the manner in which some point is suggested is very subjective, and how it is included is up to you as a minute taker. This is where experience and knowing the characters can help you, and that comes with practice.

Tip

Never be offended if the Chair or someone else asks for a correction or for you to include something that maybe you did not think important at the time. Your job is to emerge from the meeting with one version of the minutes. If they need changing from then on, so be it. It is about being professional in the same way that an editor may ask a writer to include another point in their book. This is to make the book better and is no reflection on the writer.

Difficult names

Dealing with names can be endlessly fraught. First of all, there is the capturing of the name, and then the spelling of it.

An added tension here is that names are hugely important. Our names differentiate us from each other and so are very personal (and most people also have an opinion as to whether they like their name or not). For some people, their names are a declaration of their heritage, of where they came from; for others, it is a matter of lineage – for example being given the same name as a parent. If someone calls you by the wrong name or mispronounces your name, it 'feels' somehow like they are not speaking to you, so linked are our names to ourselves. So personal are they that I have worked with people who have changed their names to better reflect their personality, and of course many pop stars decide that a change of name would better suit the image they want to project.

In fact, names are so important that, to nudge someone already quite angry or annoyed into a full-out hissy fit, you need only to refer to them by the wrong name. All this points to why we need to get it right. You would not want to be responsible for the careful negotiation turning into all-out warfare, now would you?

There are two aspects that might trip you up – spelling and pronunciation. Let's look at **spelling** first. When you are given a list of attendees, you may be given it either in writing or verbally. If it is in writing, you obviously have the advantage of everything being spelled out for you; but if it is given verbally, try to clarify any spellings (even relatively popular names like 'Smith' and 'Davis' can be spelled 'Smythe' and 'Davies' and yet be pronounced the same).

It is always better to ask someone – 'I'm sorry, can I just clarify the spelling?' – than to make a huge gaffe.

Tip

If you are unsure and you need to check up on how to spell a name, start by looking back at the past minutes. There you will find a record of previous attendees, and, if they have attended before, it should be listed.

Now let's turn to **pronunciation.** Using our example above, 'Davis' and 'Davies' are very similar in pronunciation, whereas 'Smith' or 'Smythe' could be pronounced differently – with the second version giving more emphasis on the 'y' – or not, as the case may be.

The golden rule here is to ask once and then remember – even if that means making a note as to how a name is pronounced phonetically! Nobody minds being asked how to pronounce their name initially; it is when it is then repeatedly mispronounced that it becomes annoying.

Referencing other sources and papers

On occasions, you, as minute taker, may be asked to collect or reference other details, documents or papers. For example, you may be providing administrative help (including minute taking) for a meeting in three weeks' time to discuss the feasibility of changing your power supplier. In preparation for this, the Chair may ask you to research the other leading energy companies, and obtain a business report from each so that everyone at the meeting will have the full amount of facts on each company at their fingertips during the meeting. You may also be asked to obtain some information such as when the current contract comes up for renewal, how many units the company uses, its projected usage in the future, and so on.

All of this will need to be available at the meeting (not necessarily sent out as a pre-read), and therefore you will need to ensure you have references for all sources. This can become highly important, especially if someone disagrees with the content.

If you were handed this type of research before a meeting, it might be helpful to create a reference list that looks something like the one below:

References

1. BGA Industries, *Our Power and You*, published 20XX, BGA.
2. Feature: 'Why Changing Power Matters', *Professional Facilities Manager*, no. 360, p. 30, published May 20XX, Horizon Publishing House.
3. Web download: *The Future Problems with Power*, PR Solutions, May 20XX.
4. Copy of annual facilities expenditure, contained in last year's accounts for Antics Solutions.

…with each numbered item relating to a document. This ensures that everyone has all the information to hand and you are less likely to be troubled with having to justify figures and features during the meeting. If the item remains undecided, you may also be asked to send out copies of the reports and features with the minutes, and once again these references will be helpful to everyone, enabling those that wish to to check back to the source.

Recording decisions and actions

A key section of minute taking is the recording of key decisions and actions. After all, that is primarily what the meeting is for – to either make decisions or to move projects forward towards completion.

Decisions and actions are usually either recorded at the end of each item number (on a separate line) or in a column to the right (which is left empty apart from this). The style and design is really down to you, the Chair and your organization.

Decisions and actions are usually typed in **bold** or highlighted in some way. This is simply to bring attention to them. In the busy world of work, it is very easy to miss actions (especially if you were not present at the meeting) and the minute taker needs to use all the techniques at their disposal to ensure everyone is aware of what they need to do.

Traditionally, a decision or action needs three pieces of information:

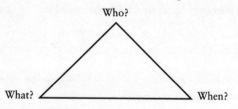

An example of this would be:

> **Action:** PP to send documents to management team by Tuesday 23 August 20XX.

or

> **Decision:** The group jointly decided to pool the money not used at Christmas to provide an outing for a local children's charity.

Some minute takers will also go over each person's copy of the minutes and highlight their actions using a highlighter pen. (This is one of the few activities that is actually easier and quicker if you are producing hard copies rather than sending a copy by email.) The reason for doing this highlighting is so that, when the person gets their copy of the minutes in the post, they can easily flick through and remind themselves of how many actions they need to take. In other words, the actions jump out, forcing the recipient to take notice. Another way of achieving the same aim would be to send the same minutes to everyone attached to an email and then copy just the names of the persons named in the action column into the main email.

Layout and numbering

If you are typing up minutes from a meeting involving a public authority such as a council, it is highly likely that there will be a complex numbering system to take into consideration. It is more than an orderly system of layers; the numbers may even refer to a highly complex cataloguing system that enables files, decisions and cases to be tracked. Where these systems are in operation, they are usually quite detailed and are set up on the computer for your text input to be inserted in the correct section.

For ordinary minutes, with a less rigid system, there may still be some layering or numbering system. The importance with any numbering system is:

▶ to know where you are
▶ to know how to get back.

Each item on the agenda will have a number. For example:

AGENDA
1 Discuss the new playground proposed for the children's area
2 Future Christmas party for the children's playgroup

Now, under Item 1 we might have discussed several issues, all a little separate – for example:

---

1 Discuss the new playground proposed for the children's area
There were several aspects to this item:
  1.1 Update on the company commissioned to build the playground
  1.2 Initial design of games and toys
2 Future Christmas party for the children's playgroup

To show that they are separate but belong to Item 1, we make them offshoots of 1 – in other words, points 1.1 and 1.2 (you could have made them (a) and (b) or roman numerals if you prefer). Now everyone is aware that when we write about Item 2 we are on a different item altogether.

However, one level may not be sufficient to order your minutes and there may be additional subsections to each of these items, and therefore it may look like this:

---

1 Discuss the new playground proposed for the children's area
There were several aspects to this item:

  1.1 Update on the company commissioned to build the playground
    1.1.1 Proposed start dates
    1.1.2 Proposed completion
  1.2 Initial design of games and toys
    1.2.1 Surface games
    1.2.2 Toys to be considered
2 Future Christmas party for the children's playgroup

Notice how we are now down to another level – 1.1.1 and 1.1.2. This way of organizing levels can be very helpful to the reader but you must remember where you are in the ordering list.

However, when the technique is mastered it can be a very effective way of ordering minutes into discrete sections and even taken further down into bullet points. For example:

---

1 Discuss the new playground proposed for the children's area
There were several aspects to this item:
  1.1 Update on the company commissioned to build the playground
    1.1.1 Proposed start dates:
      • Any time between August 20XX and October 20XX
    1.1.2 Proposed completion:
      • The job will take four weeks and therefore Sept 20XX–Nov 20XX

Action: Kara to liaise with the building company next week

1.2 Initial design of games and toys
There will be a number of free-standing toys and a variety
of games formats drawn onto the ground.
1.2.1 Surface games:
- hopscotch
- snakes and ladders
- chequers
- numbered blocks

1.2.2 Toys to be considered:
- swings
- roundabout
- see-saw

Action: Team to come up with a design and costs within budget

2 Future Christmas party for the children's playgroup

...and so forth.

Tip

Get familiar with your computer so you can set up an automatic levelling
system with the design of your choice, but you still need to tell it which
level you are at and when you need to move up a level.

KEEP IN MIND...

1 Structure is not to be shied away from – adding structure can actually help minute taking.

2 Think about writing minutes as being like telling a story or providing a narrative.

3 If anyone calls for something to be specifically minuted, do that accurately.

4 Unless you are otherwise directed, write minutes up in a formal tone, using the third person (he, she, they) and in the past tense.

5 Try to capture an overview of the issue being discussed rather than hone in on who said what.

6 Try to find out in advance of the meeting whether names are going to be an issue for you.

7 Names are hugely important – clarify and learn how to spell and pronounce each one.

8 If you find that staff members are not taking notice of the actions, try other methods to highlight them – for example adopting a larger point size, centred text, bold or italic.

9 If you have a numbering system, don't have too many layers, and make sure you can find your way back up again.

10 If using a template helps at any point in the minute-taking process, create one.

12

Writing up and distribution

In this chapter you will:
- *consider how business English is used in minutes*
- *use helpful words and phrases*
- *learn how to get minutes accepted or signed off fast.*

Procrastination – the art of putting it off

Do you prefer sitting in the meeting and taking notes or the writing-up afterwards? Some prefer the meeting because of the buzz and chatter, but others prefer the quiet time afterwards when you can order your thoughts and a product emerges. What is critical is that you encompass both parts of the activity. Notes without the completed minutes can become the hobgoblin in the corner if you are not careful, and the longer you leave them, the harder it will be to make a start.

Creating minutes is a two-part activity:

1 taking the notes, and then
2 creating the minutes.

…and, as we have seen so far, part one does not always seamlessly flow into part two!

It is so very tempting to undertake the first activity and tell yourself that the hardest part of the job is done, and that all that is left is a little typing job – but that is not really the truth and you are fooling yourself. A complex two-hour meeting could mean almost a day of typing minutes, as you wrestle with remembering the distinct points, create meaningful prose, and present it in a readable format. It is vital, when you take on the job of minute taking for a project, that you, at the same time, negotiate a reasonable typing-up and presentation time to enable you to do justice to the task. This may mean you taking yourself off somewhere quiet or working from home. It may mean other people taking your phone calls for you, and possibly other duties, while you complete the task. All this needs to be negotiated and in agreement with your manager, just in case any problems crop up later.

Now down to the task itself. I mentioned earlier that one of the key aspects with transcribing shorthand is to do it as soon as possible following the event. The same is true of minutes. Leave your notes for a week and you may be hard-pressed to even remember attending the meeting, let alone what was actually said! Therefore timeliness is essential. If you are taking minutes in a morning meeting, try to keep the afternoon clear for transcription, and if it is an afternoon meeting, try to keep the following morning clear. If you are taking minutes on a Friday afternoon and do not work weekends, I will leave it up to you as to whether you would prefer to stay at work to finish them, work over the weekend or save them for first thing on Monday morning – every organization would be different in what it would expect from staff, but you also need to think about your own powers of retention.

When situations seem challenging, or just plain hard work, it is so easy to procrastinate. 'I'll do it tomorrow when I have more time,' you say, or 'I will feel more organized tomorrow,' but of course tomorrow comes and the job seems even bigger and more difficult. Try not to fall into this trap because it will cause you to have a blockage around the situation and then you will use extreme measures to avoid it, such as reporting yourself off sick to avoid the situation entirely.

Procrastination is really about fear. You may be fearful because you want to do an excellent job, or because you know you will be judged by others – whatever it is, procrastination gets in the way and prevents you from moving forward at all. The best way to deal with procrastination is to...

▶ carve the task up into smaller sections, and then
▶ just leap in!

For example, if you are procrastinating over the minutes, tell yourself that you will just put 15 to 20 minutes aside to collect together your notes, set up a file on your computer, and type in just the top section of the minutes – just the heading and the attendees. After that you will give yourself a reward such as a cup of coffee and biscuit or piece of fruit. Before you know it, you will be thinking, 'Well, I've started now so I might as well finish the job.' You are simply tricking the brain into bypassing the very persuasive 'I'll start it in a minute' part, and leaping straight to the 'I've started so I'll finish' part.

Business English

Earlier I discussed using a more formal style and the third person and past tense to record the minutes. You also need to consider using business or formal English. This means using expressions such as 'There was considerable debate on this issue' rather than 'There was a right old rumpus over this'. You may *say* the latter but you only *write* the former. There are some stock phrases that can help you and we will look at these in the next section.

Only in the legal professions do terms such as 'hitherto' and 'notwithstanding' form normal vocabulary and therefore, unless you are in businesses where such phrases are commonplace, you need to use a regular level of business English of the kind that you see every day in business plans and reports.

If you are not clear about punctuation or grammar, there are plenty of books or sources of information for improving this area of your work, and some are suggested at the end of this book.

Dealing with swearing

There are occasions when meetings become highly emotional and swearing may occur. Do you record this or not? Do you include this in the minutes? After all, it *was* said, and it may be important.

When recording a heated exchange, it is best to capture as much as you can in the notes and deal with swear words by having a symbol or code for each word. This is for two reasons – the first is that it is faster to record this way; the second is that it is less upsetting for you as a recorder of information.

For example, writing, 'I ~ don't believe it' instead of the slightly more colourful and explicit, fuller version will save you time and be less upsetting if you are constantly exposed to bad language. When typing this up, it is up to you and your organization as to whether you fill in with the correct word or use some descriptor, for example:

> **At this point GR said, 'I [expletive] don't believe it'**

or

> **At this point GR said, 'I b***** don't believe it.'**

If you were working for any service that requires accurate evidence or verbatim minutes, you may need to type out these words in full, but it is more likely that you will leave them out – but check with the Chair (or your manager) if you are at all concerned.

Helpful words and phrases

There are two areas where you may find that you have communication anxieties:

1 when you do not hear a difficult name or catch on to a complex concept
2 trying to write minutes when you really don't understand the subject.

So, let's look at these two areas and suggest some ways around these specific issues.

There could be many reasons why you did not catch someone's name or comments. They could mumble, have a speech impediment, a strong accent, speak very quietly, hide their mouth… the list goes on. Communication is a two-way process of sending and receiving messages. Messages may be sent but it is only when they are received successfully that true communication can be said to have occurred. For example, if you were unable to understand the Russian language, there would be little point in you sitting in on a safety talk given only in Russian. You would not understand anything and therefore, although the presenter may have felt that they had communicated the safety issues to you, because you could not understand them, no communication has really taken place.

To confuse the matter further, the problem may not just be one of not receiving the message effectively. There are other barriers that can hamper effective communication such as:

▶ the assumptions of the speakers
▶ jargon and/or bureaucratic language
▶ lack of concentration (or tiredness)
▶ external influences (noise and interruptions).

In these instances, the most effective intervention is to say any of the following:

- ▶ 'Excuse me, could you repeat that?'
- ▶ 'I am afraid that this room is not the best for acoustics. Could you repeat that?'
- ▶ 'This is not my area of expertise – would you be willing to supply content on this item for the minutes later?'
- ▶ 'Can I just check this through with you again?'
- ▶ 'That was quite complex and I was wondering whether you could just put that in layperson's terms for the minutes?'

(Try to speak to the Chair in advance of the meeting if you suspect that you don't really don't understand the concepts or details being discussed. You are a valuable part of the meeting and they need you, so be assertive and ask for help or the information you want!)

Insight

If you are ever stuck, don't feel that you are in any way to blame. At meetings it regularly happens that people become a little carried away with their subjects. This is where a strong relationship between the minute taker and the Chair becomes important. In this situation, turn to the Chair and ask: 'How would you like that minuted?'

Decanting pages into sharp minutes

Another issue that causes anxieties is that of conversations going off on a tangent or there being a considerable amount of background chatter. Do you collect and include everything or sit back and try to capture just the main theme?

If you are writing verbatim minutes, you MUST try to capture as much as you possibly can, and in some instances you will not know what is important information or not until later in the meeting. To miss a factor like this could have important ramifications and therefore your default should always be to capture as much as possible. However, for most meetings an overview is all that is required. Moreover, if you take minutes for the same people regularly, you will soon get a feel for who bluffs, who is overly verbose and who takes the meeting off course, and you can work around their input.

Here are some other problems and how you might deal with them:

Behaviour	Action
Start to go into the background of the project once again	Defer to the Chair immediately, 'Do you want this background minuted?'
Spend ages on a topic and then decide not to take it forward	Summarize in one sentence – e.g. 'The team discussed the issue at length and no decision was taken.'
Start an argument	Again ask the Chair whether they would like you to capture any details, though usually this would be summarized, e.g.: 'There was an altercation, the result of which was the immediate reinstatement of the voucher scheme for staff.'

Other useful phrases are:

▶ 'There was some discord...'
▶ 'There was dissent within the group...'
▶ 'Not everyone was in agreement on the main points...'
▶ 'There was total agreement...'
▶ 'Following a lively debate...'
▶ 'The group was divided by...'
▶ 'An enjoyable half-hour was spent...'
▶ 'Jess entertained us with some background...'

Using bullets

Most people prefer minutes to be a flowing narrative of the meeting, but full minutes are not always needed, and in the case of note taking (as opposed to minute taking) in meetings, bullet points offer an efficient, effective way of sectioning information and actions. The reason for choosing bullets is that they are a fast way of giving an overview – fast for the writer and fast for the reader. Bulleted notes (like the ones here)...

▶ allow the writer to 'chunk up' information
▶ display the information in an ordered list or number of points

- can have sublists:
  - ▷ like this one
- are very quick for the reader to skim-read the main points
- can provide almost an aide-memoire list for anyone to pick up and take forward.

However, when it comes to presenting your minutes in bulleted format, check this out with the Chair before you go totally down this route. Bullet points may save you time, but, if you design the minutes on this principle and then find out later that this was not required, you could have problems tying to expand on the points later on. (It is always easier to summarize notes than to expand them again later.)

Getting minutes accepted fast

Once your minutes are complete and you have checked through for any errors, the emphasis is on getting them sent out so that everyone present can start work on their actions. Speed is of the essence here because the minutes have to be accepted (and in some cases signed) by the Chair as an accurate representation of the meeting before they can be distributed. Until they have been accepted by the Chair, they are in draft format. (This is often denoted by the word 'DRAFT' slotted into the title and which is then later removed.)

If you do not move fast on this task, you can easily find yourself in the dreadful situation of having the minutes of the last meeting still in draft format when you are ready to attend the following meeting. As the minutes have not been 'signed off' they have not been sent out, and therefore it is likely that very few people will have achieved any actions (after all, not receiving the minutes is an excellent excuse for doing nothing). You will sit in the meeting and realize that the first item on the agenda is 'Minutes of the last meeting' and your heart will sink!

When situations reach this stage, things become chaotic and the meetings themselves become ridiculed, along with the staff responsible. It is fair to point out that the Chair would also be responsible for a situation like this, but, as they are usually more senior, they often seem to sidestep any responsibility. To make sure this does not happen to you, start now by managing the situation.

I have previously mentioned fostering a close working relationship with the Chair and this becomes even more important at this time. If possible, before the meeting, agree with the Chair when they will be able to review the minutes. I have mentioned that minutes should be typed up as soon as possible following the meeting and therefore, unless there is a problem or the meeting was overly long, they should be ready at some point during the next working day. It is no good, however, if the minutes were typed up promptly but then sit in the Chair's in-box because they have gone on leave or are too busy to look at them. To avoid this, follow this quick and easy plan:

Getting minutes signed off fast is as easy as 1, 2, 3...

1   Speak with the Chair before the meeting to see when they are free to read through the draft copy of the minutes. (You may need to emphasize the need for a prompt response so that the minutes can be produced quickly – the Chair's agenda may be very different to yours and, whereas you see this as a key task, they may see it as a background task, to be done in their spare time.)

2   Be very clear and gain their agreement: 'So, if I send you the draft minutes of this meeting on Monday morning, you would be able to approve them by Monday lunchtime, so that they can be distributed. Is that right?'

3   If you find that things still remain chaotic and you are not getting the minutes back in time, manage the situation. Try: 'I realize how busy you are and therefore I would like to suggest the following. I will send you the draft minutes of this meeting on Monday morning and, at the same time, send everyone else the same set of minutes, emphasizing that they are still in draft format, and awaiting your signature. That way everyone is not waiting for the final set of minutes before starting on their actions.'

This has the practical advantage of not only sorting out the situation but also gently advising the Chair of the benefits of this more organized approach.

Corrections and learning

The Chair may make many corrections to your minutes. This is quite normal and in no way reflects the quality of your minute taking. Corrections usually fall into three clear categories:

1 **Errors** – there will be errors! You may have written a date down incorrectly or misheard some facts. It may also be that, since the meeting took place, some statistics have changed or need to be updated.

2 **Typos** – these are just the usual typos that occur when anyone is generating a document at speed. Perhaps some misspellings and/or grammatical mistakes.

3 **Style** – this is largely down to how the Chair speaks and writes. Do not be offended if a sentence is rewritten. There may be nothing wrong with your original entry but we have all seen something written and thought, 'I would not have put it like that' – and simply that is all that has happened here. Try to view this as just a quirk of the job and, if you can learn to adopt the Chair's style of writing, you will have fewer amendments to make in future.

Once they are finally signed off, your minutes are complete and they simply need to be distributed. For those who have been tasked with actions, it is always good practice to make this clear to them – either in an accompanying note or email (especially if they were not at the meeting). Before you hit the 'send' key, just make sure you have attached any presentation slides or accompanying notes.

KEEP IN MIND...

1 Taking minutes also involves typing them up and presenting them.

2 Learn to deal with procrastination and see it for what it is – just a temporary block to be overcome.

3 Use professional, business English.

4 If your minute taking requires you to deal with swear words or explicit facts, take advice on how to present this information.

5 Try to build a close working relationship with the Chair and work together as a team.

6 Set up a slick system for getting your minutes signed off and sent out fast.

7 Use bulleted minutes with care; not everyone likes them as a style.

8 Incorporate some 'stock phrases' to cover large amounts of background banter.

9 Be assertive – your job is important.

10 Don't get overly anxious about corrections, they go with the job.

Part four
Chairing meetings

13

Let's hear it for the Chair!

In this chapter you will:
- *concentrate on creating a focus for your meeting*
- *ensure all the basics are covered*
- *explore the role of the Chair and what it means to be effective.*

Generating a focus

If you have ever chaired a meeting before reading this book, you will be aware that it can be quite an onerous task. For a start, you are dealing with people and that is never easy as they will all have their individual view on matters. However daunting chairing a meeting may sound, there are tricks to making sure you are fully equipped for any situation.

Chairing a meeting implies some form of seniority (even if that is not strictly the case) and, for this reason alone, you should be running towards, rather than away, from the role of Chair. I am sure we have all been in meetings that are badly chaired, where the Chair has allowed some speakers to drivel on and cut across those trying to convey sensible points, where they have allowed the meeting to overrun and where they have not had guest speakers turn up because they had forgotten to invite them! And when these things happen, we always think: 'I wouldn't do that.' Of course, the reality is that chairing a meeting is not that easy and if you have only ever attended badly run ones, how would you know that you would do things differently?

You may not make those specific mistakes but there are plenty of others that may catch you out, as we will see through this section.

Although I cannot list every situation or instance that may threaten to confound you, I shall be covering a range of knotty issues later (in Chapter 15), and so you will be well prepared. Many people chair meetings without any training or information, but this does not mean that it is desirable. Not everyone is able to access training, but, by reading this book, you will gain valuable insights.

If you have a meeting to chair fairly soon, after reading Part four, use the section headings in each chapter as an aide-memoire together with the 'Keep in mind...' sections. They will help you to consider every angle and enable you to be fully prepared for most situations.

Some meetings will automatically have a tight focus through their very nature. However, some can appear more fragmented – a collection of items that are related only in that they concern that particular group or team. It is helpful to have a specific focus for the meeting to enable those present to...

▶ concentrate their energies
▶ work towards a joint outcome.

When considering your meeting, think in terms of an **outcome**. When you leave the meeting room what do you hope to have achieved or settled? This will be your proposed outcome that you need to implement.

To help everyone focus on the outcome, and to enable you to remind everyone to keep on track, try to state this either on the agenda or verbally at the beginning of the meeting. For example, if the meeting is primarily to decide how the new customer care scheme should be taken forward, on the agenda state:

This meeting is to discuss how the new customer care scheme should be put into operation...

and at the beginning of the meeting, as Chair, reiterate this by stating:

As you are all aware, this meeting is to discuss how the new customer care scheme will operate when it is launched. I am going to keep us all very firmly focused on this as we need a solid outcome by the end of the meeting. I will therefore have one eye firmly on the clock to ensure we cover everything, and I ask everyone to keep their points focused on resolving this issue.

Never be afraid of stating the outcome you expect and then use that focus to maintain a tight format.

Remaining practical while maintaining interest

I have never met anyone who feels that there are not enough meetings in their life; in fact, most people feel there are too many. We are all trying to achieve so much, and the modern-day workplace often has us working on several projects at once. This means that, rather than being in a traditional worker–manager (linear) situation, we may be answerable to several managers and project teams all at the same time, forming a kind of criss-cross of accountability. This 'matrix' working style means that if we have six projects, there will probably be six project meetings a month, in addition to any other meetings needed to discuss details and team meetings. Many people attend over 20 meetings a month and for some people life seems to be just a non-stop stream of meetings. It is highly likely that amid this maelstrom of discussion and talk, you will meet the same people at different meetings and some meetings will overlap or be running at the same time – in other words, as a chair, your meeting may face opposition.

We have seen earlier in the book that, if a meeting is going to be successful and move the business forward, it needs to have the right people in place who will be responsible for steering the project and these may be decision makers. If there is too much competition (whether that is because of the time slot or the subject matter), you may find that your attendees do not bother to turn up and that begins to make life very difficult for you as Chair. Suddenly you are in the situation of not achieving the meeting's aims, and every decision may have to be put on hold until the right person can make it, which may take weeks.

There are two issues here:

1 the practicality of the meeting
2 the 'tempter' or hard sell.

Let's look at each in turn.

Your meeting may be competing for a slot against other meetings, so it can be helpful to find out who else you would be up against. As Chair you might want to hold your meeting at 10 a.m. on a

Thursday but if a more senior manager is also holding their team meeting at a time that overlaps yours, and you need one of their staff to attend your meeting, that staff member is never going to attend yours – they will always defer to the more senior manager. On another practical level, if someone on the team works part-time, it would be running counter to equal opportunity legislation to hold meetings only on the days when they were not present. The message here is fairly clear in that you need to schedule meetings for when people can attend and agree that with them.

The 'tempter' or hard sell is that your meeting must make people *want* to attend. This is where having a distinct focus for the meeting is essential – but so is *communicating* it. There is little point in having a tight focus and then not letting anyone know about it. Although we still have to attend meetings, there are some that are better run and more enjoyable to go to than others. I recently heard someone say, 'Yes, I know I've got to attend but at least Kirsten is chairing it so I know it will move fast and be focused, and we will be finished by four.' Kirsten, as Chair, clearly has a great reputation, and that encourages people to attend her meetings.

Knowing your attendees

When you are in the position of Chair you need to be far more strategic in your actions, and part of this is knowing your attendees. Finding out who they are and how they react will enable you to gain additional insights.

For some meetings, you, as Chair, may not know anyone attending, and naturally, if you are chairing an open or public meeting, you may know very few people. This leaves you having to think completely on your feet and to anticipate how the different meeting attendees are going to react or behave. Unless you are highly adept at working in this way, this situation could leave you at a disadvantage. It is so much easier to chair a meeting when you know the personalities of those around the table – what is likely to make one person lose their temper or how another person is likely to feel about certain subjects. We all have 'hot buttons' that, when pressed, result in us reacting in a certain way. Being able to predict those reactions can help the Chair steer the conversation away from conflict (if appropriate) and deal with any outbursts (if necessary).

There are a number of ways to get to know your attendees:

► Seek out each person individually before the meeting and introduce yourself.
► Ask everyone (if only by email) if they have any issues or areas of contention that they would like to declare before the meeting.
► Do a little background research on each person (this might be necessary if they are from another business).
► Speak to the manager of each person attending.
► Ask around your own peer group; they may have had these people attend their own groups.

The essence here is not to probe into anyone's private life but to gain useful information that will enable you to chair the meeting more effectively.

Setting out the basics

So now you have the focus of your meeting, the time and the list of attendees. What else do you need to do?

► **Help!** – is there anyone who can help you? Do you have any support time available, perhaps in the form of an assistant or administrative officer? If you are able to access any support, whether that be to set up the meeting, help you throughout (perhaps by taking minutes), or with post-meeting activities, it would free you from the stress of running the entire process by yourself. Smaller meetings may be fine to administer on your own but larger, more complex meetings need some additional help. It is essential that you work closely with any help you are able to access. Working together as a tight team will enable you to create a seamless and smooth operation.
► **Venue** – you may use a regular room or be searching for a new one, but you need to have a venue that is large enough for everyone in the meeting to sit comfortably but not so large that there are acoustic problems and so forth. If everyone is seated too tightly, the room will become hot and the meeting atmosphere may become soporific. There is also the problem that you, as Chair, might not be able to see everyone clearly and may miss some points. You also need to ensure that the room has the appropriate amount of technical functionality you and any

guests require. Some rooms may be fully fitted with projectors and interactive whiteboards, while others may not even offer the facility of a screen.

Insight

If ever the meeting is not progressing in the way you anticipated, do consider the venue. The environment has a great effect on the mood of any meeting. Different wall colours have also been shown to have an effect on the levels of energy and motivation within the room.

▶ **The agenda** – the agenda is usually made up of:
  ▷ items you wish to raise
  ▷ items others wish to raise
  ▷ any other main business or regular features.
▶ The main business or regular features are easy to place on the agenda as they will tend to be near the beginning and the end (items such as 'Previous minutes' and 'Date of next meeting'), and that just leaves the list of items raised by you or others for discussion. As Chair, you need to know how long each item will take, so that you can calculate the length of the meeting and ascertain whether it is achievable within your time slot. (There is no point putting together an agenda that would take four hours to go through if you are basing your meeting on only a two-hour time slot.)
▶ If your agenda is too long, you have the following options – you could...
  ▷ lengthen the time of the meeting
  ▷ shorten the length of each agenda item
  ▷ reduce the agenda by removing or doubling up some items
  ▷ deal with some items in a different way (perhaps by handout or email)
  ▷ schedule a follow-on meeting shortly afterwards.
▶ The point here is that you take some form of decisive action, rather than do nothing. Also be very aware of an 'Any other business' (AOB) section tacked on the end. AOBs need to be very well policed if they are not to cause overrun problems. Do not encourage attendees to come to the meeting and just raise any subject they wish – you could be there for hours. If an item is important, it should be on the agenda and AOB should be kept for quick snippets or updates only.

Your role in the meeting

The role of the Chair is to progress the meeting in an organized manner, to maintain order, and to facilitate interaction and decision making. One minute you may be encouraging a response from someone who has trouble being heard, and the next you may be trying to rein in someone else who is being rather verbose.

Starting well before the meeting begins, the Chair needs to check that the meeting is booked in an appropriate room, ensure an agenda is created, and communicate this to whomever wishes to come or is invited. The Chair should also speak with the minute taker to clarify the type of minutes required and discuss any potential problems. At the meeting itself, you, as Chair, need to be there on time (or even a little early) to ensure the room is free and that you are available to welcome everyone.

Seat yourself in the most suitable position. You do not have to sit at the head of the table but you may feel it most appropriate to your status. If the table is round, try to avoid sitting with your back to the door as you will need to see who is arriving at, and leaving, the meeting at any given time. Your other consideration may be to sit where you can see a clock clearly for timekeeping purposes.

Once the meeting starts, your role is to...

- ▶ introduce yourself and possibly introduce others, especially at the beginning
- ▶ go through any health and safety or confidentiality issues – as appropriate to the organization
- ▶ introduce the agenda and any changes to it.

Begin by facilitating the smoothest path through the agenda, taking each item in order if possible, interjecting when appropriate, and bringing each item to a timely conclusion. Periodically you should check with the minute taker that they are comfortable and whether they need any clarification.

Towards the end of the meeting it is customary for the Chair to thank everyone for attending, set a date for any future meetings and clarify any next steps, including when the minutes will be sent out. Once out of the room, the role of the Chair is not over. A quick conversation with the minute taker will ensure that they are comfortable with their next steps, and any notes will need to be filed away. A post-meeting email reminding everyone of any urgent actions and thanking them for their input is always welcome, although not mandatory.

If the minute taker has been taking the advice in this book, the draft minutes should be ready within 48 hours of the meeting and awaiting your swift response. If possible, give this part of the process your priority as it is difficult for the minutes to be sent out without your signature or agreement. Check through the minutes immediately and concentrate on facts: Are the dates correct? Have the correct figures been quoted? – and so on. Where your writing style is different to that of the minute taker, ask yourself how much that really matters. Only rewrite if it is really necessary.

Making alliances

If your meeting is to negotiate or to decide business, rather than an open forum, you may need to consider making alliances, and also be aware of any other alliances around the table. It is almost impossible to prevent personal relationships and corridor promises entering into the bartering arena. It is quite regular business practice that, if you want someone to support your idea in a meeting or to agree with you, you visit them beforehand to sound out any opposition and perhaps persuade them to adopt your point of view.

In business you need alliances to help back up your proposals or support a weak argument. Even if you find this an uncomfortable thought, you will make alliances just through working with others and gaining their support either through your persona or your ideas. Not all alliances are deals done behind someone's back. Many are composed of people who support you just because they like your ideas, and perhaps because your ideas dovetail with another project they are heading up. Alliances can be both positive and negative. They can show solidarity in a group and instil confidence in the meeting's decisions and outcomes. However, they can also be the start of a means of pushing through unpopular decisions or staging a takeover. Be alert! As Chair, you need to feel able to identify and challenge any alliances that threaten the integrity of your meeting.

Insight

As Chair, you also have to be very aware of your own feelings concerning any of the items on the agenda, as you are in a powerful position of influence to push through, or hold back, decisions.

KEEP IN MIND...

1 As Chair you have distinct responsibilities – learn them. Don't try to be all things to all people!

2 Chairing skills can look great on your CV, so take every opportunity to practise your skills.

3 Be very clear regarding the focus of your meeting and what it aims to achieve.

4 Communicate the focus and create an inviting agenda.

5 Try to know as much as possible about the background and temperament of your attendees.

6 If you are able to engage help, do so.

7 Think through how appropriate the venue is for your meeting.

8 Be very clear regarding your role in the meeting.

9 Work very closely with the minute taker to form a tight administrative team.

10 Be aware of negative alliances that may threaten to destroy the integrity of your meeting.

14

Running the meeting

In this chapter you will:
- *consider how your own style may have an impact on how you operate as Chair*
- *learn how to draw up boundaries or a behavioural charter*
- *discover when and how to interject as necessary.*

Displaying gravitas

In Chapter 13 we looked at the role of the Chair and went through a quick résumé of all aspects of the job from beginning to end. However, the main value in having someone in a chairing role is that they lend organization and substance to the meeting itself.

The Chair is responsible for the smooth running of the meeting and is held accountable if a meeting is poorly managed. Most people have experienced meetings where the Chair appears to have no influence on the proceedings, where people feel free to accept and reply to texts, hold secondary conversations at the back, and generally appear to get away with poor behaviour. Conversely, I am sure you have also attended meetings where everything has run smoothly. Is it just a fluke or is there something we can learn from this? Part of this is skill, we know, but is there something more that we need to learn or consider?

Chairing a meeting is an important role: a role that deserves respect. To ensure you fit that role perfectly, you need to consider your own level of confidence, respect and gravitas. Why are some people instantly respected while others fight to be taken seriously? Having gravitas extends outside the meeting to your whole behaviour, but – and this is the good news – it can be developed and is not some automatic gift of nature.

First, you need to consider where you are starting from. Think back to when you have been in authoritative positions and be honest – were you the complete authoritarian or a bit of a pushover? Ruling by fear is not a good start, and neither is letting everyone take advantage of you, but there are many shades of grey in between these two polarized positions. Where are you placed? If you are unsure, ask a colleague or someone who has seen you in action. If you are too authoritarian you may need to cool it a little – otherwise you will frighten everyone rather than be composed – but if you are too laid back there may be a little tightening of the reins to be considered.

Gravitas manifests itself in your style and the way you operate. Those with gravitas have a certain presence. Although they tend to dress well, it is not just down to the clothes they wear; it is an attitude of being totally confident and in control. How do you dress when you chair a meeting? Do you feel comfortable and in control? Are you dressing appropriately for the meeting? Do your clothes make you feel confident? Everyone who chairs meetings should own one good item of clothing or jewellery. It does not matter what it is or where it comes from but it should be something that, when you wear it, makes you feel great. It will pay for itself many times over as a confidence booster!

Now, how we act. A great way to start any new set of meetings or even a meeting where you are the new Chair is to spend the first half-hour discussing how the group is going to work. Yes, you can spend some time looking at what the group will and will not cover (often called the **terms of reference**), but I am talking about behaviour here. This is not about you dictating to the group how it is going to be, but about facilitating answers from the floor as to how everyone would like the group to run... and of course you can flag up some of your own ideas, too. How about 'All phones will be turned to silent unless cleared by the Chair'? The great thing about doing this activity is that not only have you set a standard for working together, but you have also increased your own credibility through your organized action. You can keep the emerging list on a laminated flip chart and pin it up at every meeting to remind everyone of the behaviour they all signed up to – any deviation from this can be dealt with by you pointing out that the group set their own rules.

Creating clear instructions and maintaining them sets a standard that will certainly be paid back in increased gravitas, and also just happens to make the job of Chair so much easier. In essence, a double winner!

How to start

So, you have sent out a clear agenda, worked with your administrative support to set up a room with refreshments, and all the people invited have turned up except for one. You are ready to start, and you know you must start with impact – how do you now go forward in a way that demonstrates your presence?

If you took my earlier advice and arrived before everyone else you will have secured a seat in the most advantageous position, so that you can see everyone sitting clearly and also the door where everyone enters and leaves.

As each person arrives, say hello and introduce yourself to anyone you don't know, and be sure to state, 'Hello, welcome – my name is Jane Goodwin and I am the Chair this afternoon.' Try to start the meeting on time even if not everyone is present – that is their problem, and bad manners (ask the minute taker to make a note of the names of anyone missing, so that you can speak with them later). Then begin with something like...

> Hi, everyone. Thank you for coming. As you can see, we still have one or two people missing and I have one apology from Sarah Hodges who is off sick. However, we have quite a large agenda and so I am going to start and when the others arrive they can join in. My name is Jane Goodwin and I am the Customer Care Liaison Officer and I have been asked to chair these meetings. To my right is Phil Norman who is acting as administrative support for these meetings and will be taking the minutes. I think it would be useful for all of us, including Phil, if we all introduce ourselves quickly before starting.

If you have any 'rules' or 'points' you want to state, now would be a good time. For example:

> At the end of this meeting I will be arranging the date for the next meeting and therefore anyone who needs to go and fetch their

diary should do so during the scheduled break. At the moment I am thinking in terms of fortnightly meetings until the project settles down. We might then move to monthly.

Now, you are ready to move on to the items...

Thank you. Now the first item is discussing the terms of reference of the group and also creating a behavioural charter so that we can be very clear about the focus of the group discussions and also how we, as a group, would like to operate. Let's start with the terms of reference. Mark, would you like to start us off by presenting this item?

If anyone enters either during or after beginning your speech, nod an acknowledgement but do not go back and repeat everything. Make a note to ask them during the break whether they had a problem finding the room.

Taking a firm stance at the beginning and end of the meeting will go a long way in setting the tone and level of formality of the meeting.

When and how to interject

The meeting should now be off and flowing, with you in charge. However, you are not in the clear just yet. You cannot sit back; you need to be totally focused and you may have to interject now and again. There are three main reasons for you to interject:

1 You wish to move the process on.
2 You want to ask a question or clarify a point.
3 You wish to issue some warning, calm a situation down, or issue a 'red card'.

People become very excited by their own subject, which is why it can be so difficult to keep people to time. Passion can come from a personal interest, such as equal opportunities, or a deep knowledge, such as working on a project for three months. However, discussions can get heated and suddenly you are in the situation of having allowed tempers to rise and the debate to have got out of hand. When you think back you will probably realize there was a tipping point when you should have intervened, but that is easily identified in retrospect. When you are chairing a meeting in real time, it is not so easy to see the signs. Therefore it pays to take decisive action. As soon as someone begins to deviate from the original topic, you need to make a fast decision. You need to ask yourself two quick questions:

▶ Is what is being said important additional evidence for the item, or is it just posturing and words?
▶ Look at the clock – how likely is this to escalate and force the item over time?

You will have noticed that both these questions are concerned solely with the quality and timing of the item, because that is the Chair's centre of responsibility: to ensure a quality outcome, within a certain time frame.

If you decide that the conversation needs to be brought back in line, you need to resume control. Look at the following example:

I need to interject here, there is ten minutes allocated for this item, and we are already seven minutes in. Please can we come to a conclusion, and if we need to discuss the matter further, perhaps we can reallocate this item to a future agenda.

Similarly…

There is clearly a considerable amount of feeling relating to this topic. Can I suggest that it is discussed further outside of this meeting and an outcome is presented later?

It is when you need to interject to issue a warning or calm a situation down that any agreed collective set of behaviours (as discussed in the following section) really comes into its own. If you have done this simple activity earlier, then you only have to refer to them in this situation:

Excuse me, everyone, but I would like to draw your attention to the list we produced earlier regarding behaviour and how we wish to respect each other. I think this might be the most appropriate time to call a ten-minute break while we all think about our own behaviour, and then get back to business.

Two things are happening in that example. The first is that you are asserting your authority by interjecting, and the second is that, by calling a break, you are giving each party some time to calm down (and expecting them to do so), before moving on. It also gives you the opportunity to speak to each party in the break if necessary, and to try to calm them down individually.

Timekeeping and rules

We humans do tend to fall into one of two camps: those for whom timekeeping is of the utmost importance, and those that regard the time of a meeting as nothing more than a vague indication of when they should arrive. Unfortunately every workplace will have a mixture of each type, so it is highly likely that you will also have a mix of each within your meeting. The problem is, though, that, whereas some things in life can be loose and informal, meetings do have to run to time, and, even if someone has a problem with that, it is only good manners for them to try to accept others' need for timeliness. In this sense, meetings are similar to the railways. You cannot run an effective rail network if you are sloppy about timings – trains would be constantly crashing into each other and no one would be clear about when to arrive. Without a time framework your meeting would be equally as disastrous.

Try to encourage everyone to attend on time by reminding them regularly that you will start on time, no matter who is present, and that you also intend finishing on time. Try to choose a time and venue that everyone can access easily (so there is no excuse for not being able to find it or for someone to blame the lack of parking), and even send out a welcome note with the agenda asking everyone to be punctual. It is also best practice to detail all timings in the minutes, together with who enters or leaves the room, and the time that this happens. This is so that anyone reading the notes can see instantly who was in the room when each decision was made. However, it also serves to identify latecomers. If someone is habitually late to a regular meeting, it might be worth speaking with them or their manager to find out what the problem might be, and whether you can help by moving the time of the meeting.

In previous sections I have suggested that you may want to create some terms of reference for the meeting. This just means a set of statements outlining the parameters of the meeting and its raison d'être – 'reason for being'. I also suggested drawing up a behavioural charter to set out how the group will behave towards each other – for example, 'Everyone is free to challenge', 'Mutual respect for all contributions', and so forth. In addition to these you may also want to set some rules such as 'The meeting will always finish by 5 p.m.', 'All mobile phones to be switched off' or 'All attendees should make every attempt to be on time for each meeting'.

Don't make too many rules, and try to keep matters light, but a behavioural charter can help in the case of any conflict, especially if the perpetrator was originally part of the group that signed up to it.

Tip

The membership of some meetings fluctuates. If that is the case, you will need to quickly run through any terms of reference, behavioural charter or rules and ask whether they have any issues with these, since they were not involved in their original formulation. If they accept them, they too will be held to these documents, and will have to work within their parameters.

Keeping the agenda moving

Your aim is to keep the agenda moving and take each item in turn. However real life is not always that simple. Perhaps the person presenting one of the items is delayed or will not be able to attend. As Chair, you will need to reorder the agenda on the go.

The first question you need to ask is whether the person is just late, or not attending at all. If they are going to be late, and it is possible to move the agenda contents around a little, the situation may just need some quick and judicious thought (such as whether the item feeds into another item and therefore needs to be presented before that other item).

If the person is unable to attend at all, you need to enquire whether anyone else is free to present in their place. If the answer to that is 'no', you will need to move the agenda item to the following meeting. The point here is to keep the agenda fluid and moving. I have already discussed the importance of time, but the need to present a flowing agenda that moves from one item to the other seamlessly and efficiently is also very important.

Remember! As Chair, you are the facilitator of the process, and unless you are stepping in for another Chair who could not make it, your agenda should be set so that it flows, and so that, where necessary, topics build on each other. There is no point having an item at the end that has a massive effect on all previous items when it should have been presented first. If you find part way through that the agenda is ordered incorrectly, speak with your minute taker and then state:

> *I will be taking the agenda items in a slightly different order because, on reflection, it would be better to discuss the team reorganization (Item 6) before the other items in case it changes those responsible for actions. The agenda will thus be taken as Items 6, 1, 2, 3, 4, 5 and 7.*

Although you want to keep the agenda moving smoothly, do consider the needs of your minute taker. They will need regular breaks. In some organizations they have dual minute takers so that they alternate in 30-minute blocks. This is because the role of the minute taker is extremely tiring.

Raising energy levels

In meetings you can feel the energy, and that can be up or down. Sometimes it is due to the **subject matter** and other times it may be the **environment**. This is not about fun and games, but meetings have to engage and have an energy that provokes ideas.

Starting with the environment, and based on the premise that there are some things you can control, consider your meeting room. If you are assigned a room and have no choice, then fine, but if you do have a choice – where would be the most energizing? Consider these factors:

- ▶ **Decor** – brown is a very lacklustre colour, and red can cause irritation, so how about clear or pastel colours?
- ▶ **Lighting** – try to adjust the lighting to be as natural as possible.
- ▶ **Seating** – too comfortable and everyone will fall asleep, too stiff and there will be complaints after an hour of sitting.
- ▶ **Heating / air conditioning** – too warm and again there will be drooping eyelids; too cold and attendees will be sitting in their coats.
- ▶ **Food** – food is not always good before a meeting as it tends to have a soporific effect. If food is essential but you need lively minds, have the meeting first and food afterwards.
- ▶ **Drink** – have plenty available – but make it water!

Now for the subject matter. You cannot be responsible for what is on the agenda – business is business – but you can think about *how* items can be presented. On the agenda, if it does not interfere with the flow, have a presentation followed by a discussion, for variety. If things look like they are seriously sagging – perhaps in the middle of an all-afternoon meeting – first send everyone out for a five-minute comfort break to get everyone moving. Now put people into teams when they come back so that they can work together in small groups of three, four or five people, and feed their thoughts back via the group. Whenever you get people to move or group differently, you will re-energize them and their ideas will be much more creative in content.

Accommodating disability

As Chair you also need to be sensitive towards any member with a disability attending the meeting. It is important to note that some people do not consider themselves to have a disability, as with the correct level of support, they are able to undertake as many tasks as any other person. This, therefore, can be a sensitive area. In addition, different disabilities require a variety of provisions: some will need additional equipment to be set up (such as a hearing loop system); some involve facilitating access such as allowing more space for a wheelchair or reserving a space by the door, while others may require you to accommodate an additional place for a carer.

If you do not know the person concerned, it can be helpful to contact them prior to the meeting to discuss the facilities that are available and to enquire whether there are any other additional adjustments that could be made to ensure that the meeting is able to go ahead in comfort for them.

Tip
If you are unable to speak with the person direct, prior to the meeting, contact either an occupational health professional (some organizations have their own) or a disability awareness group and ask for guidance.

KEEP IN MIND...

1 Act like the leader you are in this situation.

2 Take control by speaking first and discussing boundaries and the agenda.

3 Make a firm start by introducing yourself and your team.

4 If you need to interject, do so assertively, but politely.

5 To calm a situation down, suggest an early break.

6 As Chair you have every justification to speak to anyone who has continual issues with managing their time.

7 Try to make the most of the time you have by keeping the agenda moving along.

8 It is OK to take items out of order as long as you explain what you are doing.

9 Build in a break or change every 40 to 60 minutes – your minute taker will love you.

10 Make every effort to accommodate any attendee with a special need or disability.

15

....

Troubleshooting

In this chapter you will:
- *cover a range of problems and issues, ensuring that you are always ready*
- *consider body language and how that can help in meetings*
- *gain awareness of the ethical issues surrounding some requests.*

Problems, problems...

It would be lovely to think that you will now sail swiftly through your working life, chairing meetings and having no difficulty, but of course things are bound to slip you up. People will fail to turn up or be awkward, computers won't compute and projectors refuse to project. Such is life in the real world – mostly totally unpredictable – but it is good to have some ideas hidden away in your memory bank just in case things do go wrong.

In meetings all kinds of things can happen and what I hope to cover here are just some of the more regular questions I am asked, together with my responses. This may not cover every eventuality but it will certainly give you a good grounding in avoiding major pitfalls and should provide some guidance for the future.

It has to be said that some problems are avoidable and would not have occurred had you planned effectively or considered a contingency option early on. However, there is also the utterly out-of-the-blue problem that will always catch you unawares, and for which you could never have planned – unless you've read this book, of course! Let's look at some examples.

Organizational problems

▶ **Agenda not sent out** – this is more common than you may think. Perhaps you were responsible for it and you forgot or maybe it is an administrative error – whatever, the important thing now is to get things back on track. Pay no attention to blame, and do not mention any fault within the message, simply email out an agenda immediately with your sincere apologies and ask for any last-minute entries. The second most important action is to make sure that everyone is attending because the agenda may have been their reminder to put the meeting in their diary. If there is an insufficient number of people, you may have to reschedule the meeting, but if everyone is able to attend, carry on with a flourish... and make a diary note for next time! This is one of those instances where the less fuss is made, the soonest it is forgotten.

▶ **Papers not sent out** – this is similar to the problem above but not quite so worrying in that the people attending will at least have the date in their diaries. The worst is that they will come unprepared. If papers can be emailed, they can be sent out up to the night before. If they need posting, they can be sent by courier. Failing this, they can be made available on the day, but naturally they will not have been read in advance.

▶ **Venue not confirmed / is double-booked** – even if the room is in your building, if you know other people use it, try to get a confirmation in writing. It looks very unprofessional if, when your guests arrive, you then have to spend the first ten minutes of the meeting trying to find another venue because someone has double-booked or it is needed by another team. Most workplaces will operate some form of booking procedure. If you truly are caught in a double-booking situation and there are no other rooms in the building, consider local hotels and motels (both their conference rooms and coffee lounges), local cafés and so forth. Even schools, care homes and religious buildings often have free rooms that are available for hire.

▶ **No refreshments** – you are part way through a meeting and are waiting for the refreshments to arrive... but they don't. There has clearly been a glitch somewhere in the booking system and no refreshments have been ordered. What should you do? Go ahead with a comfort break and, while everyone is stretching, try to find a pitcher of water and some glasses or paper cups. This will help considerably as most people are more concerned about drinking than eating. If you are able to make hot drinks, you could make them for everyone while seeing whether there is an administrative assistant nearby who could help you in investigating the problem. If you promised lunch would be included in the meeting, then you may be able to take everyone out, or you could buy some sandwiches in from a nearby café.

▶ **No minute taker available** – if you know about this in advance of the meeting, you may decide to reschedule. It is very difficult to be both Chair and minute taker and, if you are not confident that you can do both roles, I would advise you not to attempt it as there is the danger that you may do both badly. You could hire a minute taker from any temping agency, but, if you do so, build in time for explaining the background to the meeting, so that they are aware of the context. You could record the meeting but be warned that you cannot always identify voices clearly from a recording. If you find that there is no minute taker on the day (perhaps the person has phoned in sick), then either you can ask for a volunteer from the meeting (attendees could take it in turns) or ask each owner of each item to write up their own minute notes, just for their item. You can then merge them all together and review them, after the meeting.

▶ **The fire alarm goes off / the building is evacuated** – many meetings start with attendees filling in a signing-in sheet (stating who is present), and an explanation of fire and safety rules. If you hear a fire bell or need to evacuate, pick up the sheet and ask everyone to exit via the correct exit, leaving their bags and papers behind. Follow the last person out, and bring the list with you. If anyone is missing (perhaps they went to the toilet), tell someone immediately. Don't go looking for them as they may have left the building via another route.

Technical problems

▶ **The computer is not working** – you open up your laptop and your presentation fails to load. If you were prepared, you should have at least one copy of the presentation in paper format with you. You could ask for it to be copied and work from the paper. If you had another copy on a digital stick, there is a high possibility that someone else will have a computer or device that you can load your presentation on to, just for today.

▶ **No projection screen** – not all rooms have a built-in full-size screen. First, is there a fairly flat, non-patterned wall? Even if the wall is not beige or white, and is a little uneven, it should take a projection successfully – you may just need to change the background colour of your slides. (If this is a constant problem for you, it is possible to buy fairly inexpensive portable screens that either can be attached to the wall or have their own stand.)

▶ **No power points in the room** – first check the amount of power left in your computer. If you have sufficient, that is one less thing to worry about. Try to contact the facilities department – there may be hidden sockets somewhere in the room (sometimes they are built into the facia). If you really do need power, you will have to trail an extension lead from another room, but if you do this, make sure, of course, that it is well signposted – for health and safety reasons.

▶ **No light-dimming capability** – this can be a problem for presentations. Not all rooms have ambient lighting options and in some rooms the light is simply either on or off. If that is the case and you need reduced lighting, are there any blinds or curtains you can draw? If there is nothing, keep the lights on (if you need them to see everyone) during the main meeting and switch them off only for the presentation.

▶ **Wrong version of software** – older operating systems often do not support more modern software. You may have the latest version at home but not realize that a large company may be at least one version behind (because it costs so much to update hundreds of computers). As this is something that has actually happened to me, I always bring my own laptop with me. Always ensure you have another version of your presentation on a digital stick or disk, and a paper copy – just in case.

▶ **There are microphone issues** – if you are chairing a large meeting you may need to wear or use a microphone. Gossiping and going to the restroom with it still turned on are two of the most obvious areas to try and avoid – many famous people have been caught out by gossiping while their microphone was still turned on. If you need to use a microphone, practise, and remember to turn it off (or remove it fully) when you finish speaking.

People problems

▶ **Key people need to leave early** – if their item, or their input for other items, is crucial for today, rejig the agenda to bring those items forward so that you can deal with as much as possible before they go. If this is not possible, consider calling a separate meeting to deal specifically with these issues.

▶ **People talking at the back** – if you find this happening, pause the meeting and then say, 'I am afraid I cannot hear you for the background noise. Can I please ask for quiet while others are speaking.' If it continues, call a five-minute break and speak to those concerned. If it continues after that, ask them to leave and for that to be minuted – you can feed back to their manager later. If this is an issue that has been happening regularly and not been dealt with, either change the layout of the room or move to a room with a round table (no corners to hide in) and use nameplates, either splitting offenders up or placing them nearer the front.

▶ **Key speaker does not turn up** – beforehand, ring them if possible to find out if they are on their way. If they are late, you can usually reorder the agenda to place them a little later, but, if not, you have the choice of either rescheduling or asking them to send through their presentation slides and undertaking it yourself (if you understand the subject).

▶ **No volunteers for actions** – so no one wants to volunteer? What a surprise! In the first instance, and depending on the situation, you may want to try to coax potential people by offering to remove some part of their other work to accommodate the task in question. If that does not work, or you prefer a more direct approach, remind them of how this task links to others that are crucial for the department and how developmental the task would be, then suggest a name and offer support. For example:

> *Obviously I am disappointed that no one appears to want to do this particular project. The outcome of this could seal the fate of the department in the future, and, although it is not an easy project, it offers a heavy dose of development which any of you could then put on your CV. What about you, Helen? You've often said that you would like to try something more strategic? There will be a lot of support available.*

(If the Chair is sufficiently senior, they may allocate jobs rather than ask for volunteers.)

▶ **One person hogging the stage** – be quite direct and say, 'I would like to hear from some other people now. Carol, Pete – what do you think?' Or, 'I think we are all very clear on your view, Vincent, and I would like to hear from the others.' If it is a recurring problem, speak to the person about their behaviour. They may not realize that it is so noticeable.

▶ **Speakers over their time limit** – do not feel bad about interrupting them. Speaking to a time limit is a skill and one that everyone who presents needs to learn. You can tell, from what they are saying, whether they are near the end (summing up) or in full flow. If they are about to sum up, allow them to finish but step in and state:

> I'm afraid there is no more time for questions because we are right up against the clock now. If you have a question for Mr Latimer, please speak to him in the next break.

If they are in full flow, intervene with:

> I am sorry to interrupt you, Mr Latimer, but it is my job to keep the meeting to time and we are already running late. Could I ask you to sum up quickly? We will try to catch up the time by shortening the break.

▶ **Too many people speaking at once** – this can be annoying and if you can control this with one mention, then fine. However, if it persists, it can be irritating for everyone and you will find that little progress is being made. One idea that may seem playful (but which actually works) is 'holding the stick'. Bring in a short baton and announce to everyone in the meeting that only the person holding the baton can speak. At first people will laugh but, as they find that they are frustrated because they want to speak over the other person and can't because they are not holding the baton, it will become evident to them how intrusive their behaviour was to the even flow of the meeting.

Behavioural issues

▶ **Causing a fracas** – nip this in the bud before it gets out of hand. Thinking that someone will suddenly change is a mistake; if someone is demonstrating bad behaviour they need to be told that this is not acceptable, but not in such a way that demeans or exposes them. If you see the temperature rising, call a halt to proceedings and ask the main protagonist to join you outside for a moment. When outside, explain that this behaviour is not acceptable, and not the best way of resolving any dispute, and give them the option to either return to the group, or to leave now.

▶ **Using mobile phones** – start each meeting by asking everyone to put their phone on silent unless they have special dispensation from you to leave it on. If you stipulate this upfront, you are less likely to have a problem later.

▶ **Sniggering and/or jeering** – people who snigger or jeer from the side often do not have the confidence to go public. Halt the main speaker and look at the protagonist directly. Say, 'I'm sorry, do you have something to add to the last point?' or 'Clearly you have feelings about this situation; would you like to state them so that everyone can hear?' Putting them on the spot can stop this behaviour in its tracks.

▶ **People entering part way through** – again this depends on the situation. If they had travel problems or are the speaker you were waiting for, you may feel grateful that they arrived at all! However, if they are perpetually late, ask the minute taker to make a note of the interruption and the time. Speak to the person afterwards and publish their late attendance in the minutes. If your attendees are late, resist the urge to keep going back over the 'story so far' unless it's vital to the meeting – it is intensely annoying for everyone else present. Tell them that you will bring them up to speed at the first break or provide a résumé afterwards.

▶ **People leaving the meeting part way through** – if someone is genuinely rushing off to another meeting and has explained this beforehand, then this may be acceptable. However, if this is a recurring event, tackle them directly as in the previous point.

▶ **Person taking over** – there is often one person who has rather a lot to say on the subject. You may think that they are loud and forceful but they often view themselves as just taking part and contributing. This means that this problem can be one of perception. Speak to them privately and bring this behaviour to their attention – they may not realize how it is being perceived – and suggest some other ways for them to contribute a little less forcefully.

▶ **Sitting back and not taking part** – it can be difficult when you want everyone to contribute to find someone sitting back. You need to make a judgement here – is their lack of contribution because they are bored (or not engaged), or is it because they are shy. If they are shy, it might be better to seek them out later and find out their views, but if it is because of them disassociating themselves from the meeting, offer a challenge. Ask: 'We have not heard from Bob. You are unnaturally quiet this afternoon, Bob; what are your views on this subject?'

Don't minute that!

What do you do when someone says, 'Don't minute that!'? You have a judgement to make here – was the information disclosed valuable to the meeting or argument, or was it superfluous piffle? Was it emotional comment or a fact? For example, if someone makes a well-meaning joke, 'Well, he would say that, wouldn't he? – Oops, don't minute that!', there is no need for the comment to be minuted. It is superfluous and non-threatening. However, if someone said, 'I know for a fact that he has money hidden in a Swiss bank, but we had better not minute that,' you may feel that this is quite important information and that it needs to be noted so that things could be taken forward if necessary and, if anything does happen in the future because of this situation, you are all covered.

This also applies to actions. If someone becomes angry and bangs their fist on the table to make a point, there is no need to minute that action. However, if the same person bangs their fist into someone else (who may later make a complaint), the incident should be minuted.

As Chair, you may also ask the minute taker not to minute certain situations or actions. You have two opportunities to do this, in the room, or later when you read through the minutes to sign them off, prior to distribution.

If you are finding that behaviour is becoming difficult or you anticipate behavioural issues at a meeting, start off with creating a behavioural charter I mentioned earlier to try and discourage this type of outburst.

Body language

Many of the behavioural problems we have looked at in this chapter can be anticipated through the Chair keeping a close watch on body language. Very occasionally you will meet someone with such a mercurial temper that you do not see the outburst coming, but, in most instances, tension starts to build before the outburst, and that is manifested through body language. I mentioned earlier that it is useful to know something about how your attendees behave or if there are any items that may excite them *before* the meeting. You can do this by getting to know them and their work, and observing them in other meetings. You will find that, although body language is not the same for everyone (for example, not everyone, when they are irritated, pushes their chair back, folds their arms and juts their chin up), people are remarkably consistent. Learning these nuances comes from people watching and paying attention to even the smallest movements, perhaps the fists tightening, hand-to-face gestures such as earring twiddling or beard/chin stroking, or small muscles in the face and neck tensing up or, in extreme cases, twitching. These could all be early warning signs that tempers are escalating.

Insight

Look out for early signs and, as Chair, you are in the perfect place to step in to try and defuse the situation. Call a break in proceedings, remind the participants of the importance of maintaining professionalism, allow for some cooling-off time, or, if absolutely necessary, defer the item or indeed the entire meeting.

Pay attention to your own body language, too. What signals are you sending out and how helpful are they in the situation unfolding in front of you?

KEEP IN MIND...

1 Try to remedy any situation immediately – leaving it will only make it worse.

2 Everyone forgets something sometimes, so do not be too hard on yourself or others.

3 Some behaviours are unconscious, and people only need to be made aware of them for them to stop.

4 Keep in mind that most situations, if they go off track, are redeemable if you can just keep your cool.

5 Do not be afraid to be strong and assertive regarding behaviour. Others in the meeting will look to the Chair to give firm guidance.

6 When attendees leave or join part way through the meeting, it is a disruption. If you have not been forewarned, then you may need to speak to them about this.

7 Using mobile phones and texting during meetings need to be kept in check as they are very rude behaviours. Ask for phones to be set to silent and build in a five-minute comfort break in which attendees can pick up their messages.

8 Learn to deal with poor behaviour from others. The stronger your reputation as someone who does not suffer fools gladly, the easier it will be for you to act decisively in meetings in the future.

9 Make sure that *you* are the judge of whether a comment or action is minuted or not.

10 Become acutely aware of body language and use that knowledge to judge feelings and tension in the room.

16

....

Ending the meeting productively

In this chapter you will learn how to:
- *consider how to bring the meeting to a productive conclusion*
- *increase the chances of minuted actions being completed*
- *build rapport and improve relationships with the people you meet in meetings.*

How to bring the meeting to a conclusion

The meeting is over and, in the sudden relief that you managed to achieve all your aims and move items along successfully to completion, you must not forget that there is work still to be done. The meeting may indeed be over but there is a considerable amount of consolidation tasks to be undertaken.

The role of the Chair continues after the meeting has ended, and therefore so does the responsibility. As Chair, your name will be linked with the meeting and in some instances (such as public meetings) you may even find that the Chair will be congratulated (or otherwise) on the way they handled the meeting. As your reputation partly relies on the word of other people, it is best to ensure that you follow all procedures so that you cannot be faulted on format, even if your style needs improvement.

It is also important to remember that the people attending your meeting have given up valuable time to attend, time that they could have given to another project, and they need recognition for that. Hopefully your meeting will have some solid outcomes and therefore everyone will consider it well worth their time attending. However, it is not always like this, of course. I expect we have all attended meetings where the outcome is somewhat ambiguous and you wondered why you bothered to attend – after all, you have loads to do back at your workplace. So, let's look at how to complete the meeting in a genuine and positive way.

The meeting needs to come to a definite conclusion and that can be expressed in a number of ways, depending on the success of the negotiation or items covered. As Chair, you need to assert your role in bringing the meeting to a close. A weak 'Um, is that it?' does not leave a lasting impression of someone who has run the meeting like a conductor runs an orchestra. It sounds indecisive and unassertive; all your earlier achievements in conducting the meeting could be wiped out in an instant! Instead, make a strong statement such as:

> Well, everyone, that seems to bring us to the end of our items for this meeting.

This is definite and leaves no one in any doubt that you are about to 'wrap up'. Not only does this statement sound conclusive but it is also *inclusive*; the use of the term 'everyone' tells those present that this was a shared experience.

Setting future actions and summarizing

Following on from the completion of the main body of the meeting, you may wish to build in a summarizing section. Summarizing is important because it enables everyone to…

- ▶ reflect on the amount of ground the meeting has covered
- ▶ think about the decisions that were made
- ▶ confirm that they are happy about the outcome of each item.

As Chair, when summarizing, you need to be providing an overview of each item in approximately one minute per item. This can also be really helpful for the minute taker because it also provides them with an overview of the item for their minutes, too. It provides an opportunity for them to clarify any difficult names or details once again.

Do be aware that very occasionally summarizing can open up the initial issue once again and someone who was unhappy with the original result may try to pick up the point once again. They may even have been planning their comments through the previous items and waiting for just such a moment as this. It helps to be ready just in case this happens. Think on your feet and consider:

- ▶ Did I give the original item sufficient 'air time'?
- ▶ Is the speaker just wanting to voice, yet again, that they are unhappy about the outcome?
- ▶ Are they simply making a point or do they have something new to bring to the table?
- ▶ Is this the same point or something completely different?

...then decide whether you should allow them to continue or move decisively to bring the conversation to an end. It may be that you decide to allow them to continue or schedule the item to appear again at the next meeting.

Together with the summary it can also be helpful to go through the actions, and clarify any dates (including the date of the next meeting). The greater emphasis you place on actions, the more likely they are to be completed.

For example, instead of saying:

OK, I would just like to go through everyone's actions before we leave. John you said that 12 October would be OK for the report, and Sylvia, you are going to get the details to John by 5 October. Pete, you are going to find out about the new building for the meeting on 10 October and you will also check with Fran that she is available to take the minutes that day. OK, everyone, let's go.

...try:

OK, let's check those actions to see that they are all possible. You have all had time to reflect on the dates and I want to just check that they are all possible so that you don't commit yourselves to unrealistic deadlines. John, you said that 12 October would be possible for the report – is that a reasonable date? Sylvia, is the 5th reasonable for that information? Pete...

Checking dates out with each person on an individual basis may take a little longer but they are more likely to be given priority and achieved because individuals have agreed to undertake the tasks in front of others.

Thanking everyone for their input

I mentioned earlier that many people give up their time to attend meetings. Just because people have been told to attend a meeting does not mean that they go with a happy outlook and willing to contribute. They may still be reluctant to attend, and contrive to find other excuses to avoid actually attending. If they feel unappreciated or that their contribution was not valued in the past, they may attend but not completely engage in the meeting. Even the most tedious meetings have been salvaged by having great personalities around the table.

The Chair has quite a significant role to play in creating and maintaining ambience before, during and after the meeting. In the same way that you may have identified certain managers who you would prefer to work with, there will be certain Chairs who are recognized as being more pleasant to work with.

An easy method for winning 'hearts and minds' is to thank everyone fully for attending and for their input. This should take place at least twice, but ideally three times. The thank you should be at the end of the meeting. Just before everyone disappears, it is helpful for the Chair to simply say, 'I would just like to thank everyone for coming today and also for their input. It has all been greatly valued. Thank you.' A second (and perhaps a little more personal) opportunity occurs when you are walking back to your workspace or when you are walking through an open-plan workspace and you recognize someone from the meeting. Just a simple 'Thanks, Jan, for attending. I think it really went well, and your input was great,' can really lift the spirits. Of course, you will have the opportunity of seeing everyone outside the meeting. In some instances, though, attendees might disappear into taxis and you may not see them again. The third opportunity is to send a thank-you email when you are back at your workstation. Everyone loves to receive a thank you, and a short message such as 'Thanks for everything today, Tom – really good meeting' is all you really need. If you treat people well, it won't be long until you are receiving feedback that your meetings achieve a greater percentage of attendance than others, and this equates to more energy in pushing the project forward.

Picking up on behavioural issues

I mentioned earlier that behavioural issues need to be picked up outside of the main meeting. In most cases it is the job of the Chair to do this, particularly if they are the ones that form the focus of the attack or have a particular problem with that behaviour.

What type of behaviour are we discussing here? I am thinking in terms of someone being downright rude to another person during the meeting, perhaps swearing or using inappropriate language and/or gestures, butting in or speaking over someone else, or even perhaps ignoring you or disrespecting your role.

We talked about confronting the person directly during the meeting, but whether you chose to do this or not, you will still need to speak with them (and possibly their manager) afterwards. However you choose to tackle this, the rule applies that sooner is better than later. It is very difficult to contact someone and say, 'I wanted to speak with you because your behaviour at the meeting last month was appalling.' They will just say, 'Really? I don't even remember,' leaving you picking an argument over memory rather than facts. Far better to say, 'Ah, Gary, I wanted to speak with you about your behaviour this morning and ask what you meant by it?' Now Gary feels more cornered and is more likely to be responsive.

The important issue here is that you are not speaking to Gary to tear him off a strip; you have not tried to blame him. What you have requested is an *explanation* (if one is needed) and you have intimated that you will be wanting a change in behaviour for the future. As Chair, you don't need Gary to feel contrite; you need him to see that his behaviour either did not achieve anything or that it caused problems. It is important to be firm but fair. To make Gary aware of the situation as you saw it, you need to…

▶ explain the problem
▶ offer him the chance to explain or apologize
▶ tell him that if you encounter such behaviour again he will not be welcome in your meetings
▶ offer him the chance to change.

Not everyone is willing to change, and if Gary has to be replaced in the meetings by a colleague, then that is his choice, and he will have to live with the repercussions of that choice.

If you are not firm, Gary, and others like him, will create havoc at every opportunity in meetings where you are the Chair as they will know that you are weak in that role and that they can get away with this behaviour. The strong Chair is not someone who shouts and lays down the law; it is the person who tackles issues quietly and decisively behind the scenes.

Processing the minutes

If you are lucky to have had the attendance of a minute taker, you may be feeling that the job has been done for you. Well, in a way it has, but not all of it! Your minute taker will have taken down as much information as they were able within the space of the meeting, but they cannot know everything you are about to discuss, and the background to every topic.

> **Insight**
>
> If you are using a freelance minute taker, try to free up some time before the meeting to provide them with background information. It can be nerve-racking going into a meeting to take minutes when you don't understand the topic, and it will save you time later by you having fewer corrections to make.

Even experienced minute takers can be thrown by unusual topics and therefore try to establish a working relationship with your minute taker before you begin. If possible, they should be seated beside you so that both of you can confer if there is an issue, and there should be a clock or timepiece in view.

Important advice for meetings with harrowing content

Depending on your area of work, some meetings may contain content that is quite distressing (for example, stories of abuse and recounting of incidents of torture or murder). Those who are part of the meeting are often oblivious to the fact that the minute taker may not be from that same area of work and is possibly finding the whole situation harrowing. Where this is the case, it is vital that you, as Chair, debrief and speak to the minute taker before they leave the building. If they need to drive home, or back to the office, just make sure that they feel able to drive safely, and perhaps give them your phone number (or that of a counsellor, if your organization employs one) if they feel the need to speak about the content later.

Following the meeting, and after thanking the minute taker, ask them when you might expect the minutes in draft format. (If you are a manager or hold a senior position, you may find that you can use your seniority to arrange for some free time so that the minutes can be completed quickly.) The faster the minutes go out, the more effective you look and the sooner everyone can start on their actions. (Although it is not strictly necessary to have the minutes in your hand before you start on actions, not having them is the most common excuse for why actions have not been achieved.)

From your point of view you need to check the minutes above all for accuracy. However, inevitably style comes into the equation. In truth, we want everyone to write and express themselves as we do, but if you are going to rewrite the minutes on every occasion, not only will that take you too much time but it is also highly demotivating for the minute taker. If you do not like the way that the minutes are presented, discuss that with the minute taker and coach them into adopting something like your style, but do not expect them to phrase every sentence as you would. The questions you need to concentrate on are:

▶ Are all the facts correct?
▶ Do the minutes present an overview of the main points of the meeting?
▶ Are they presented in the company format?
▶ Are everyone's actions clear?

As long as the answers to each of these questions is 'yes', your minutes can be signed (or agreed) by you, and be sent out.

Follow-up

You will need to decide how much follow-up you intend to do. If you are a project manager, and the meeting is monthly, it is highly unlikely that you would wait for each month to come around before you check out how the actions are progressing. It is more likely that you would look people up, ring or drop by to monitor progress. This follow-up results in you feeling more 'on the ball' and up to date with how the project is progressing and whether the actions are taking place.

Your follow-up may also take the form of a progress report or a midway meeting. We have all heard the jokes about holding a pre-meeting meeting, but in some organizations this is necessary, as leaving everything until the meeting itself is too high-risk.

Finally, we have talked about actions but only those of others around the table. In reality, *you* may also have actions to undertake following the meeting. If this is so, make sure you set aside time in your diary to achieve them. It does not look good if you expect others to achieve actions but you have not managed to achieve your own!

Try this: a little reflection
Before you tear off to chair another meeting, take a little time out to reflect on how you chaired this one. Ask yourself honestly whether you could have improved your performance in any area, and whether there are things you would change, if it were possible to run through it again.

Make a note of any of those ideas either in the back of this book or make it part of an exercise that forms evidence of continuing professional development (CPD), something that is so often required for your career. We can all improve, and reflecting on our past performance can create a great base for the improved future performance that accompanies personal growth and learning.

If you feel there are still areas that require improvement, write them into your appraisal, personal development plan or future goals so that you can work on them during the year.

KEEP IN MIND...

1 Your meeting should end on a definite note.

2 The meeting may be over but your responsibility is not.

3 How you chair meetings is a reflection of you as a manager.

4 No matter how mandatory a meeting is, people have given up time to attend and therefore you owe it to them to make the meeting as productive as possible.

5 Don't be afraid to pin people down in the meeting to ensure they understand their actions and commit to them publicly.

6 Always thank everyone for their input and work – not just once but at least twice.

7 If someone has a behavioural issue, do not ignore it – speak with them as soon as possible.

8 The minutes need to be processed as soon as possible so give them priority.

9 Concentrate on checking the facts shown in the minutes and be less vigorous about style.

10 There may be follow-up work to undertake as a result of the meeting or to progress for the next meeting. Do not see the meeting as an end in itself, more like a continuous flow.

Taking it further

Helpful sources – websites

www.ehow.com – advice on how to take minutes in a meeting

www.growingu.com – for programmes on assertiveness

www.meetings.org – notes on chairing meetings

www.negotiation.org.uk – notes on chairing meetings

www.plainenglish.co.uk – the campaign for plain English in all forms of communication. This website has a wealth of information and exercises.

www.rescourcecentre.org.uk – for downloadable PDF files on chairing meetings and taking minutes

Further reading

General:

Mastering Meetings: Discovering the Hidden Potential of Effective Business by The 3M Meeting Management Team (McGraw-Hill, 1994)

Making Meetings Work in a Week by Graham Wilcocks and Steve Morris (Hodder & Stoughton Ltd, 2000)

Meeting and Event Planning for Dummies by Sue Friedmann (John Wiley & Sons, 2003)

Meetings by H. Parry (Croner Management Skills Guides, 1994)

Taking Minutes of Meetings by Fiona Gutman (Kogan Page, 2010) (and eBook)

Self-confidence and presentation:

Be More Confident: Teach Yourself by Paul Jenner (Hodder Education, 2011) (and Kindle)

Building Self-Confidence for Dummies by Kay Burton (For Dummies, 2011) (and Kindle)

Present with Impact and Confidence: Teach Yourself by Amanda Vickers and Steve Bavister (Hodder Education, 2010) (and Kindle)

How to Feel Confident: Simple Tools for Instant Confidence by Leil Lowndes (Harper Element, 2009) (eBook)

Self-Confidence: The Remarkable Truth of Why a Small Change Can Make a Big Difference by Paul McGee (Capstone, 2009)

Presentation & Communication Skills by Lynda Byron (NuBooks, 2011) (eBook)

Speed reading:

Work Smarter with Speed Reading: Teach Yourself by Tina Konstant (Hodder Education, 2010) (and Kindle)

Successful Speed Reading: Flash by Tina Konstant (Hodder Education, 2010) (and Kindle)

Meetings – Speed Reads by Maria Pemberton and Helen Rice (Directory of Social Change, 2009)

Management:

A Guide to Better Management: Effective Meetings by John Allen (and Kindle)

Running Meetings: Expert Solutions to Everyday Challenges, Pocket Mentor series (Harvard Business School, 2006) (and Kindle)

Facilitating Meetings and Chairing Discussions by Julia Rowan (NuBooks, 2011) (eBook)

How to Make Meetings More Productive by Pete Harmon (www.ebookboxs.com, 2009) (and Kindle)

Business English and writing:

Better Business English: Executive Writing Skills for Managers by Fiona Talbot (Kogan Page, 2009)

Better Business English: How to Write Effective Business English by Fiona Talbot (Kogan Page, 2009)

Can Do Writing: Proven Ten-Step System for Fast and Effective

Business Writing by Daniel Graham and Judith Graham (Wiley, 2009) (and eBook)

The Language of Business Meetings by Michael Hanford (Cambridge University Press, 2010) (eBook)

Some Essential Grammar Tips for More Effective Business Writing by Natalie Canavor and Claire Meirowitz (FT Press, 2010) (eBook)

Helpful contacts

American Institute of Management – www.americaninstituteofmanagement.com

Chartered Institute of Personnel and Development – www.cipd.co.uk

Chartered Management Institute – www.managers.org.uk

Institute of Administrative Management – www.instam.org

International Association of Administrative Professionals – www.iaap-hq.org

International School of Management – www.ism.edu

International Project Managers Association – www.ipma.ch

Project Management Institute – www.pmi.org

Training – www.karenmannering.co.uk

Index